CA

D064577

NO LONGER PROPERTY OF
SEATTLE PUBLIC LIBRARY

Hong Kong

Hong Kong

BY BARBARA A. SOMERVILL

Enchantment of the World™
Second Series

CHILDREN'S PRESS®

An Imprint of Scholastic Inc.

Frontispiece: **Hong Kong skyline**

Consultant: Ho-fung Hung, PhD, Associate Professor, Department of Sociology, Johns Hopkins University, Baltimore, Maryland
Please note: All statistics are as up-to-date as possible at the time of publication.

Book production by The Design Lab

Library of Congress Cataloging-in-Publication Data
Somervill, Barbara A.
  Hong Kong / by Barbara A. Somervill.
     pages cm. — (Enchantment of the world)
  Includes bibliographical references and index.
  ISBN 978-0-531-21698-9 (library binding)
1. Hong Kong (China)—Juvenile literature. I. Title.
  DS796.H74S66 2015
  951.25—dc23   2015000525

No part of this publication may be reproduced in whole or in part, or stored in a retrieval system, or transmitted in any form or by any means, electronic, mechanical, photocopying, recording, or otherwise, without written permission of the publisher. For information regarding permission, write to Scholastic Inc., 557 Broadway, New York, NY 10012.
© 2016 by Scholastic Inc.

All rights reserved. Published in 2016 by Children's Press, an imprint of Scholastic Inc.
Printed in the United States of America 113

SCHOLASTIC, CHILDREN'S PRESS, and associated logos are trademarks and/or registered trademarks of Scholastic Inc.
1 2 3 4 5 6 7 8 9 10 R 25 24 23 22 21 20 19 18 17 16

Statue, Po Lin Monastery, Lantau Island

Contents

Left to right: **Lantau Island, dragon boat races, Chinese Lunar New Year, Lion Rock, Tian Tan Buddha**

CHAPTER 1

At the Market

CHEN JINXING IS VISITING HER MOTHER'S RELATIVES in Hong Kong, a crowded region of southeastern China. Like many teenagers, she enjoys shopping, and she has come to the right place. When it comes to finding a deal, buying something unique, or browsing through shops, few places can compare with Hong Kong.

Hong Kong's markets are so varied and interesting, they are as much entertainment as they are shopping places. Jinxing's cousins heard that there is to be a Cantonese opera at Temple Street Night Market this evening, and that is something that can't be missed. Goods sold at the Temple Street Night Market may not always be top quality, but it is hard to pass up the atmosphere.

Opposite: **The Temple Street Night Market is sometimes called the Men's Street because it specializes in goods such as men's clothing and men's watches.**

Traditionally, Chinese names have the family name first and the individual's name second. A person named Cheung Yan-su, for example, is Mr. Cheung. In Hong Kong, however, it is not unusual to find someone with an English name and a Chinese name, such as Henry Lee or Alison Wong. On official records, such as Hong Kong Identity cards, the family name is printed first in all capital letters. It is followed by the person's other names. So, officially, Sarah Mei-ling Leung would appear as LEUNG Sarah Mei-ling.

A fortune-teller looks at a customer's palm. The practice of trying to tell a person's future by looking at the lines in a hand dates back more than two thousand years.

The teens' first stop is a fortune-teller's stall. Here, Jinxing can have her face or her palm read, or she can have a caged white finch pull her fortune from a pile of cards. Choosing to have her palm read, Jinxing discovers that her future will include travel and a rewarding career.

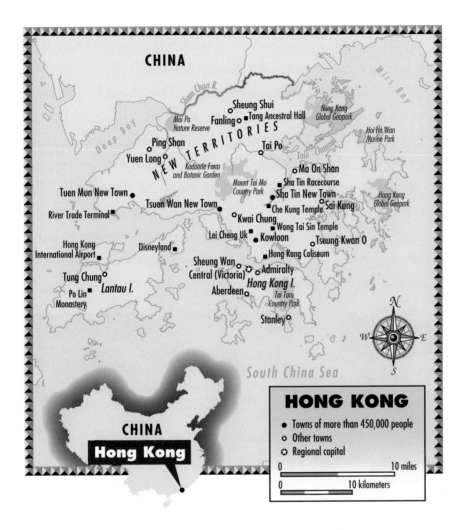

A block away, a singing group is presenting Cantonese opera. This particular show is a *Mou* play—an opera with martial arts. The Mou Sang (male warrior) is in conflict with the Dou Maa Daan (young female warrior). Musicians play *bangzi* (drum), string, and woodwind instruments to accompany the singers. This performance involves more acrobatics than acting, and the audience laughs, sighs, and applauds the opera. They also put money in a basket on the ground. It is only fair to pay for such a fine performance.

Jinxing and her cousins are hungry. They head to a noodle shop on Reclamation Street. The food is excellent, although eating it can be a little messy. As they eat, customers spit anything inedible back on the table. Jinxing orders tossed noodles with roasted duck. Like the diners at other tables, she spits out the bones.

Finally, the teens get down to serious shopping. Jinxing needs sunglasses, a dress, and a leather belt. At each stall, she picks through the merchandise. She knows that everything is

Noodle shops line the streets of Hong Kong.

Jade is a green rock that has been valued as a carving material for thousands of years.

overpriced and plans to bargain the shop owners down to a reasonable price. She gets a great deal on the sunglasses and a 40 percent discount on a sundress. The leather merchant wants more than she is willing to pay, so she passes up the belt.

While they are in Kowloon, the teens decide to visit the Jade Market. This is a group of more than four hundred jade sellers who offer everything from carvings and statues to jewelry and raw jade pieces. Jade merchants shout to draw the

The Language of Hong Kong

Although Hong Kong was under British rule for many years, Cantonese Chinese is the most common language. Many people speak both languages. Chinese is a character-based language, which does not translate well into the alphabet used in English. Here is a guide to help in pronouncing the names of people and places in this book.

Letter Pronunciation

a	sounds like "ah" as in "rah"
c	sounds like "ts" at the end of "hats"
i	sounds like "ee" as in "bee"
q	sounds like "ch" as in "chip"
u	sounds like "oo" as in "too"
x	sounds like "sh" as in "shoe"
z	sounds like "ds" at the end of "beads"
zh	sounds like "dr" as in "drew"

girls' attention. Jinxing's mother collects jade figurines, and Jinxing finds the perfect piece—a delicately carved jade butterfly. It is expensive, and she cannot talk the seller down to what she can afford, but he has a solution. He has a slightly smaller, simpler butterfly in a pale green shade. It is not as delicate as Jinxing's first choice, but it is beautiful. Haggling over price begins again, and Jinxing leaves with a smile and a lovely jade butterfly pendant.

It is nearly midnight, and the teens catch the bus home. They'll sleep until noon, and then head out to visit some of Hong Kong's other unique markets. The Goldfish Market is literally swimming with goldfish of every size. Some of the fish at the Goldfish Market are rare and expensive, costing as much as several thousand Hong Kong dollars.

The official name of the Hong Kong region is the Hong Kong Special Administrative Region (HKSAR or SAR). It is not a country by itself but a part of the People's Republic of China. The region is referred to as both Hong Kong and the SAR. Hong Kong Island is one part of the SAR. So, Hong Kong is a region, an island, and a city.

Jinxing wants to visit the Bird Garden. This is the place to buy songbirds, mynah birds, rare larks, and whistling thrushes. Many elderly Hong Kong men bring their own birds to the Bird Garden for a bit of fresh air and a song. Jinxing splurges on a handmade bamboo cage, although she has no idea how she will get it home to Guangdong, a region farther north. Now, all she needs is the right songbird!

A boy holds a green parrot in the Bird Garden, where thousands of birds and cages are for sale.

CHAPTER 2

On the Edge of China

THE HONG KONG SPECIAL ADMINISTRATIVE REGION, or the SAR, is located in southeastern China. The SAR is governed differently from the rest of China because it was a British territory for many years. In 1997, Great Britain returned Hong Kong to China's control, but some of the old ways continue. The SAR includes 261 islands that are larger than 5,400 square feet (500 square meters) as well as several peninsulas that jut out from the mainland, including Kowloon, Sai Kung, Wan Tsai, and Clear Water Bay Peninsulas. The total area of the SAR is 427 square miles (1,105 square kilometers), which is slightly smaller than the city of Los Angeles, California.

Opposite: **The Hong Kong coastline has many sandy beaches that nestle between the mountains and the sea.**

The Lay of the Land

The SAR is divided into three sections: Hong Kong Island, Kowloon, and the New Territories, which include the outlying islands. By area, the largest region is the New Territories. Kowloon is the flattest and the most built up.

The rugged coast of Cape D'Aguilar is protected as a marine preserve.

Hong Kong Island is the second-largest island in the SAR. Although Hong Kong is known for its densely populated city, it also has surprising wilderness. Part of the Wanshan Archipelago, or chain of islands, Hong Kong Island has a ragged coastline and a center covered with hills. Victoria Peak, in the west, is the island's highest point at 1,811 feet (552 m). The area around Victoria Peak is mostly parkland. Tai Tam Country Park stretches across much of southeastern Hong Kong Island. The park includes small streams, gentle waterfalls, hiking trails, and a large reservoir that provides much of the island's water supply. A winding ridge called Dragon's Back runs along the southeastern corner of Hong Kong Island. It is an area of sweeping landscapes, steep slopes, and isolated beaches. At the southern tip of the island lies Cape D'Aguilar, a region known for its striking rock formations and plentiful marine life.

Hong Kong's Geographic Features

Area: 427 square miles (1,105 sq km)

Largest City (2011 est.): Kowloon, population 2,108,419

Highest Elevation: Mount Tai Mo, 3,140 feet (957 m)

Lowest Elevation: Sea level along the coastline

Number of Outlying Islands: 261 (over 5,400 square feet or 500 sq m)

Largest Island: Lantau Island, 57 square miles (148 sq km)

Longest River: Sham Chun, 23 miles (37 km)

Largest Lake: Inspiration Lake (artificial), 30 acres (12 ha)

Tallest Waterfall: Long Falls, 115 feet (35 m)

Largest National Park: Hong Kong Global Geopark, 19 square miles (50 sq km)

Average Daily High Temperature: 64°F (18°C) in January; 90°F (32°C) in July

Average Daily Low Temperature: 57°F (14°C) in January; 79°F (26°C) in July

Average Annual Precipitation: 94 inches (239 cm)

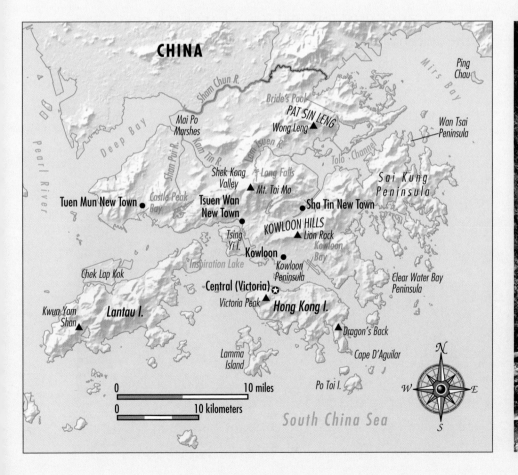

Kowloon lies on the mainland, a short ferry ride across Victoria Harbour from Hong Kong Island. Kowloon's overall area has increased during the past century as engineers have reclaimed land in both Victoria Harbour and Kowloon Bay. The southern part of Kowloon is flat and heavily populated. To the north, a ridge of mountains surrounds Kowloon's border. This includes Lion Rock, a thin strip of mountains filled with thick forests, scavenging birds, eagles' nests, and cheeky primates. The black-eared kite is a scavenger that feeds on animal carcasses, dead fish, and trash. Lion Rock's macaques are the descendants of pets released by their owners during the

Lion Rock Country Park, in the New Territories, is a popular hiking spot.

1920s. They are aggressive, and visitors are warned to keep a safe distance away from the macaques.

The New Territories have not been "new" since the 1800s. However, the name has stuck. The New Territories cover nearly 90 percent of the SAR's territory. The northern boundary is the Sham Chun River. In the south, the New Territories back up against Kowloon's northern border and spread eastward to small peninsulas touching Tai Long Bay. The west runs up to Deep Bay and the wetlands of Mai Po Nature Reserve. Most of the mountainous areas of the New Territories are part of country parks.

The outlying islands are considered part of the New Territories. The largest of these islands is Lantau, at the mouth of the Pearl River. Lantau is the nation's largest island, nearly twice the size of Hong Kong Island. Lantau is mostly mountainous, and more than half its area is devoted to parks and hiking trails.

Lantau Island is one of the least developed parts of Hong Kong.

Mount Tai Mo

Mount Tai Mo (Big Hat Mountain), which lies on the mainland of the New Territories, is the SAR's highest peak at 3,140 feet (957 m). The mountain is an extinct volcano, formed millions of years ago. Small cracks called hot pots reach deep beneath the mountain and vent warm air. Local residents call this warm air "dragon's breath." Mount Tai Mo is noted for its orchids, tall bamboo, and tree ferns. When the Japanese occupied Hong Kong during World War II, most trees on Tai Mo were cut down. Since then, trees have been planted on Mount Tai Mo's slopes, and new forests have grown.

Shan and Leng

The SAR sits atop ancient, extinct volcanoes. A crescent of hills, ridges, and mountains stretches from the northeast to the southwest. Translated from Chinese, *shan* means "mountain," and *leng* means "ridge." Most mountains in Hong Kong are fairly short, with the tallest being Tai Mo Shan, or Mount Tai Mo, which rises to 3,140 feet (957 m). Wong Leng, a peak in the Pat Sin Leng mountain range in the New Territories, is a typical height of a Hong Kong ridge. It reaches 2,096 feet (639 m) high.

Although Hong Kong's peaks are volcanic, no eruptions have occurred for many years. There has been, however, a recent discovery of an extinct supervolcano. The massive volcano last exploded 140 million years ago, spouting enough ash to cover all of Hong Kong. Hexagonal columns of volcanic rock on islands in southeastern Hong Kong are the remains of this great eruption.

Hong Kong's Waters

The SAR has few rivers and natural lakes. The region's largest lake is a reservoir, or artificial lake. Inspiration Lake, which is on the site of Hong Kong's Disneyland, covers 30 acres (12 hectares). The lake is used for both recreation and irrigation. Smaller lakes in Hong Kong include Bride's Pool, Mirror Pool, Po Chu Tam, and Lecky Youth Pool. Bride's Pool pours into several waterfalls. Mirror Pool sits at the top of a hillside and feeds a beautiful waterfall.

The dramatic columns of volcanic rock in southeastern Hong Kong formed when lava cooled and then contracted in a uniform way, breaking the rock along clear lines.

The Sham Chun River
separates Hong Kong from
the rest of China before
flowing into Deep Bay.

The longest river in the SAR is the Sham Chun, which marks the border between China and the New Territories. Other major rivers are the Ho Chung, the Kau To Hang, the Shan Pui, the Lam Tsuen, and the Kam Tin. These rivers begin in the mountains of the New Territories and flow into the SAR's harbors. To prevent flooding in the cities and towns through which the rivers pass, the government has built canals, levees, and channels to control the water's flow. Some of these channels, such as the Tai Hang and the Wong Nai Chung, flow through underground nullahs, storm drains that help prevent flooding.

Many rivers, streams, and nullahs in the SAR are polluted. The SAR's large population, poor disposal of industrial waste, and erosion of topsoil contribute to serious pollution in the water supply. Hong Kong's Environmental Protection Department (EPD) is working to find ways to control water pollution.

Hot and Humid

The climate in the SAR is subtropical. This means hot, sticky, rainy summers and cool, dry winters. Hong Kong has four well-defined seasons. Winter (December to February) is dry and cold, but sunny. Don't expect any snow unless it is on Mount Tai Mo. Spring (March to May) offers gradually warmer days and cool nights, with increasing amounts of rain as the season moves into May. Summer (June to August) is just plain hot. The daytime temperature usually reaches 90 degrees Fahrenheit (32 degrees Celsius), but high humidity

A car drives through flooded streets following a typhoon in 2012.

Typhoon Warning System

Hong Kong weather forecasters keep a close eye on any typhoons that might strike the SAR. When a number 1 warning is issued, a typhoon is nearby, and people should expect wind and rain. A number 3 warning means to expect strong winds. A number 8 warning means go home! When a number 8 is announced, all businesses, schools, and nonessential activities in the SAR stop. Everyone goes home to wait out the storm.

Hong Kong's forests turn brilliant oranges and yellows in the autumn.

makes it feel much hotter. Autumn (September to November) is the best time for a visit, with rainfall lessening, temperatures becoming more comfortable, and Hong Kong's many maples painting the landscape red with their changing leaves.

On average, about 94 inches (239 centimeters) of rain fall on Hong Kong each year. Spring and summer bring heavy rainfall. June is the rainiest month, with an average of about 18 inches (46 cm) falling. In summer and early fall, severe storms called tropical cyclones or typhoons sometimes strike the SAR. By October, the rain slacks off, and the weather is beautiful. January and February see the least rainfall, with only one or two rainy days each month. Ping Chau, an island in the northwestern part of the SAR, is the driest region, averaging 55 inches (140 cm) of rainfall yearly. The highest average rainfall is 118 inches (300 cm) yearly near Mount Tai Mo.

Looking at Hong Kong's Urban Areas

The SAR is not divided up into cities. Instead, it is governed as a single unit. But the region does have different urban areas. Some have been settled for hundreds of years, while others are only a few decades old.

With a population of 2,108,419 in 2011, Kowloon (right) is one of the SAR's most heavily populated areas. It is a financial and shopping district. Among Kowloon's main sights are the Kowloon Walled City, Sung Wong Toi Park, and Holy Trinity Cathedral. Kowloon City's public market is one of the largest markets in the SAR.

Central, sometimes called Victoria, is second in population, with 992,221 people. It is the administrative capital of the region.

Tsuen Wan New Town (below), which has a population of 801,800, is one of nine new towns developed since 1973 to cope with the SAR's growing population. An industrial center, Tsuen Wan New Town is located in the western part of the new territories.

Sha Tin New Town, which now has a population of about 630,000, was once a rural town of about

30,000 people. Sha Tin is built on land reclaimed from Tolo Harbour in the eastern New Territories.

Tuen Mun New Town, with a population of 470,900, is built on land reclaimed from Castle Peak Bay and on area valleys and hillsides in the western New Territories. The SAR's River Trade Terminal handles bulk cargo in Tuen Mun. Although the settlement is primarily residential, there are also minor industries in Tuen Mun.

CHAPTER 3

Wild Wonders

CHUN QI BO IS DOING A STUDY OF SPECIES DIVERSITY for her biology class. She plans to base her research on the Mai Po Marshes, a sprawling wetland at the end of Deep Bay, at the northern edge of the SAR. Mai Po will provide plenty of material for Qi.

She begins by doing a bird survey in the fall. Many migratory birds stop to rest in Mai Po. Qi photographs as many different bird species as she can. Later, she will use a birdwatcher's guidebook to identify any species she does not know. Right away, she recognizes the black-faced spoonbill, an endangered species. She spies an oriental stork and a black-headed ibis, both dipping their beaks in the water to catch fish. Two Dalmatian pelicans float past on the pond. Although she is concentrating on birds, Qi spots a pangolin—much like an armadillo—sunning itself on a grassy bank, and she snaps a photo. Today was a good start. Qi noted more than seventy bird species and one mammal, the pangolin. She will need to come back several

Opposite: **Great white egrets, curlew sandpipers, and red-necked stints share the water at the Mai Po Marshes.**

Pangolins

Pangolins are unusual creatures that are armored with overlapping scales for protection. When threatened, pangolins role themselves into tight balls. Relatives of anteaters, the pangolin has a long, muscular, sticky tongue that it uses to gobble up ants and termites. The pangolin has no teeth, so instead it eats small stones that help grind up its food.

times to identify as many of the four hundred bird species and other wildlife of the Mai Po marshes as possible.

On the Wing

More than five hundred bird species live at least part of the year in the forests and wetlands of Hong Kong. Most are migratory birds that pass through in spring and fall or live there during the winter.

Bird-watchers flock to wetlands where about 250 different species of water and wading birds might gather. Colorful Mandarin ducks and red-crested pochards nest near tundra swans. Gray herons dip their beaks in the water to catch fish, beside Malaysian night herons, oriental storks, black-faced spoonbills, and black-headed ibises.

Pelicans enjoy the salt marshes and the coastal waters, along with several other interesting seabirds. Great cormorants and shearwaters dive for fish in Mirs Bay. Sandpipers and curlews skitter across in the sand, leaving behind their distinct footprints. Overhead, black-tailed gulls and whiskered terns soar on ocean breezes while they hunt for food.

Hong Kong's raptors range from tiny Amur falcons to midsized ospreys and large imperial eagles. Among the more unusual birds of prey are the black baza and the besra. A small bird with a black-and-white striped chest, the baza feeds mainly on insects. Besras are midsized hunters that feed on lizards, dragonflies, and rodents.

The SAR's woodlands are full of songbirds, and many of these birds are common only in Asia or Africa. There are more than a dozen varieties of thrushes, as well as many war-blers, cisticolas, and prinias. Hong Kong is also home to more than thirty species of flycatchers.

The eastern imperial eagle is a powerful predator. It hunts hares, squirrels, and other small mammals as well as a wide variety of birds, including ducks and crows.

Tiny Flyer

The scarlet pygmy dragonfly is extremely small as dragonflies go. Its total body length is about 0.6 inches (1.5 cm). This bright red insect makes its home in freshwater swamps or reservoirs. When the sun is high in the sky, the dragonfly assumes a perfectly vertical position to help keep the sun off most of it so that it won't get too hot.

More than two hundred species of butterflies are seen in Hong Kong, including the common birdwing butterfly.

Birds are not Hong Kong's only winged creatures. Bats make up nearly half of all mammal species in Hong Kong. The short-nosed fruit bat roosts under Chinese fan palm trees. Tiny Japanese pipistrelles feast on about three thousand mos-

quito-sized insects every night. Hong Kong even has a fish-eating bat, the Rickett's big-footed bat! The area also has about two hundred species of butterflies and more than one hundred species of dragonflies.

Mammals

Hong Kong's largest mammal is the wild pig. These critters are a serious problem, particularly to the region's farms. They damage crops and destroy lawns and gardens. They feed on anything, and Hong Kongers are warned never to feed the pigs and to use strong fences to protect their crops.

Other than humans, the SAR has only three types of primates: rhesus macaques, long-tailed macaques, and hybrid macaques. Because the rhesus and long-tailed macaques live in the same area, crossbreeding has occurred, producing hybrid macaques. An area of Kowloon Hills is so overrun with the macaques that it is called Monkey Hill.

Some of the region's mammals are native only to Asia. Leopard cats are small and spotted, only distantly related to large leopards. Leopard cats hunt a wide range of animals, including lizards, birds, rats, mice, and, occasionally, farm chickens. Masked palm civets are related to weasels and mon-

A girl feeds chips to a group of wild macaques on Monkey Hill. Nearly two thousand macaques live in the region.

gooses. They are ground dwellers that hunt rodents, snakes, and frogs. Chinese ferret badgers live in grasslands and hunt insects, frogs, snails, and rodents. Muntjacs (barking deer) feed on both plants and animals, eating grass, fruit, seeds, bird

Muntjacs are sometimes called barking deer because they emit sharp barking sounds to warn other animals of danger.

eggs, and even small mammals. The males have tiny antlers and tusks, which they use to fiercely protect their territories.

Reptiles and Amphibians

Hong Kong is home to eighty-seven species of reptiles and twenty-four species of amphibians. Scientists continue to discover new species of reptiles and amphibians as they explore deeper in the forests and mountains of Hong Kong. Five species of sea turtles and six species of freshwater turtles swim in Hong Kong's waters. Tree lizards, skinks, and geckos live in the forests and beside small streams.

A wide range of snakes, many of them venomous, are found in Hong Kong. Spine-bellied sea snakes, banded sea snakes, banded kraits, and coral snakes are among the most dangerous snakes in the region. Some Chinese eat snake soup, and some people capture infant snakes and raise them for food.

A man working in a snake shop in Hong Kong holds a cobra. The snake shops sell the animals to restaurants that want the freshest possible meat for their snake soup.

Species in Danger: Romer's Tree Frog

Romer's tree frog lives only on Lantau, Lamma, Chek Lap Kok, and Po Toi Islands in Hong Kong. It lives in forests and near streams and wetlands. With a length of between 0.6 and 1 inch (1.5 and 2.5 cm), it would be easy to overlook this tiny, brown, spotted frog. Adults hunt at night and feed on termites, crickets, and spiders. When a new airport was built in 1992, nearly two hundred frogs were saved, bred, and moved to eight sites to start new populations. The frogs established themselves in seven of the eight locations and continue to breed.

In Local Waters

In the waters around Hong Kong, tropical fish are plentiful. The local waters support more than eighty species of coral.

A Hong Kong man sells his catch of the day.

Hoi Ha Wan Marine Park

Hoi Ha Wan Marine Park is Hong Kong's greatest success in protecting sea life. The park protects a bay on the Sai Kung Peninsula in the eastern part of the New Territories. At the park, divers and snorkelers can view sixty types of coral and 120 species of reef fish. At low tide, tips of coral peek up out of the water. A close look reveals sponges, anemone shrimp (left), sea cucumbers, and Chinese damselfish thriving on the reef. Spiky black sea urchins create a dark sea floor on which no human wants to step. Large chocolate hinds blend in well with the rocky sea floor, and gobies guard the burrows of local shrimp. Hoi Ha Wan is a top attraction for Hong Kongers.

Reefs made of coral skeletons are breeding grounds for fish, crustaceans, nudibranchs, and sea slugs. Clams and oysters cling to reefs while octopi creep over the sandy seafloor looking for a meal. Shrimps and crabs, brittle stars, and sea urchins are common and heavily fished.

Many fisheries and reefs in the area are in trouble. Hong Kongers eat nearly every edible sea creature. As a result, many species have been overfished. To help restore the fisheries, conservationists are building artificial reefs and stocking them with newly hatched fish. So far, more than 220 species, including groupers, breams, and snappers, are using the artificial reefs for shelter and nurseries. Restocking has improved the numbers of abalone, prawns, crabs, and sea urchins. Efforts to control the pollution of freshwater streams, wetlands, and coastal water are also having a positive impact.

Pink Dolphins

Some dolphins seen around Hong Kong have a pink tinge to them. They are Chinese white dolphins. At birth, these dolphins have black skin, which fades to gray, and then to white. The dolphins' pink color comes from blood vessels near the skin's surface. Chinese white dolphins live in the Pearl River Delta, where they feed on the abundant fish. Their population is small (about 1,200), and they are protected by the government.

Forests and Flowers

For many years, Hong Kongers cut down their forests because they needed timber for building and wood for heating and cooking fuel. A program of reforestation began with pines, mainly because they grew quickly. Recently, reforestation programs planted tree species native to the region, including maples, yews, mountain date palms, and Faber's oaks. Hong Kong dogwoods also now cover the woodlands, blooming with white and pink flowers in the spring.

On the mountainsides, rhododendrons paint the landscape red and pink. Orchids add to the purple-pink color scheme. Camellias grow on small evergreen trees and produce small, bright red flowers. Azaleas and crape myrtles add even more shades of pink and rose to the hillsides.

In the wetlands, Hong Kong iris and balsam add deep purple and bright yellow to the green of bird's-nest ferns, tree ferns, and wetlands reeds. Mangrove trees sprout at the bor-

der between fresh water and salt water. Their knobby knees stick up above the waterline. In freshwater ponds, pale Indian lotuses emerge from the water on thin stems.

Salt water will kill most plants, but mangrove trees thrive in it.

Kadoorie Farm and Botanic Garden

In the 1950s, Lord Lawrence Kadoorie and Sir Horace Kadoorie founded the Kadoorie Farm and Botanic Garden in the foothills northwest of Mount Tai Mo Country Park. Originally, the place was designed to help Chinese immigrants learn how to farm in the New Territories. Today, the site is a tourist attraction, a nursery, and more. Winding up the road toward the peak of Kwun Yam Shan, visitors pass fields full of organic crops. Greenhouses protect the many tropical flowers grown at Kadoorie. The site also includes a butterfly garden, a deer park, and a large enclosure for birds. Injured raptors undergo medical care and rehabilitation at the raptor roost. Kadoorie also grows tea and medicinal herbs available for purchase.

The National Flower: Bauhinia

Hong Kong's flag features a white, five-petaled Hong Kong bauhinia, a species of orchid. The bauhinia family consists of two hundred species of pink or purplish-red flowers that grow on trees. The aromatic flowers measure from 4 to 6 inches (10 to 15 cm) across. Only a handful of bauhinia species produce white flowers.

Conservation and the Environment

Hong Kong's government recognizes that a large population in such a small area requires careful management of natural resources. In addition to the programs that are in place to regrow forestland, there are several nature preserves and nature refuges to safeguard areas for wild plants and animals. In the rugged mountains, old forest is more secure because it is difficult to build or farm on that land.

Only about one-quarter of the land in Hong Kong is developed. Beautiful forests thrive on much of the rest of the land.

Hikers explore the beautiful coastline of Lantau Island.

Hong Kong protects all birds, bats, cetaceans, and many mammals, reptiles, and amphibians. Killing one of these animals results in fines of up to five million Hong Kong dollars, which is more than six hundred thousand U.S. dollars. Many native plants also fall under government protection.

The government is also encouraging ecotourism as a way of protecting the environment. Many travelers to Hong Kong want to enjoy its natural splendor. They take trips out to sea to spy dolphins and visit the region's many nature preserves and parks to hike trails that take them through Hong Kong's unique natural world.

CHAPTER 4

Through the Years

Hong Kong's history dates back thousands of years. About 4000 BCE, Stone Age settlers moved into the area while hunting for food. The sea was a rich source of fish, oysters, and clams. The forests provided nuts and berries, and wood for fires or for building huts. Over the next two thousand years, settlers established permanent villages along the coast.

Opposite: **The Hong Kong region has a long human history. This model of a house was found in a tomb that dates back about two thousand years.**

Early Peoples

Archaeologists, scientists who study the remains of ancient people, have found stone tools, pottery, and spearheads that provide clues about how these early people lived. By about two thousand years ago, people were using bronze to forge better weapons and tools. They made axes for cutting down trees or defending themselves from attacks, and fishhooks to help catch food. Since bronze was first developed in the Middle East, the region where Africa and Asia meet, some trade between the two regions must have existed. It was most likely sea trading because the rugged hills behind what is now Kowloon and the New Territories would have been difficult to cross.

During the Qin dynasty (221–206 BCE) and the Han dynasty (206 BCE–220 CE) people began to move from farther north in China into Kowloon and Hong Kong. The evidence of this migration includes coins, metalwork, and other household tools. In 1955, the untouched brick tomb of Lei Cheng Uk was found in Kowloon. Inside the tomb, archaeologists discovered Han-period funeral furniture, pottery, iron tools,

A container found in the Lei Cheng Uk tomb. This tomb is the only Han-era tomb in Hong Kong.

and bronze goods. The tomb provided key evidence about death rites of the Han Chinese.

In the 1200s, the Mongol leader Kublai Khan and his army swept southward over China. A family of Han Chinese fled before the Mongols arrived and settled in the far south, in what is Hong Kong today. The Han clan was the first Chinese group to create a major settlement in the region. Over the years, more people sought safety in the south. The Tang clan settled in the Shek Kong Valley, and the Hau, Pang, Liu, and Man moved into what is now the New Territories. These clans are known as the five great clans.

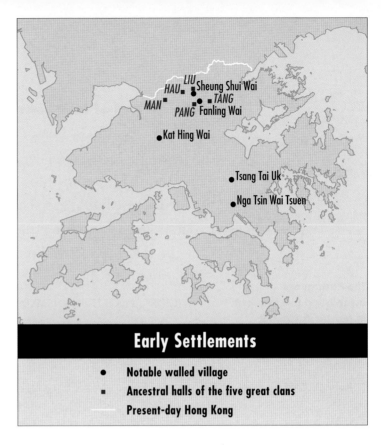

Early Settlements

- **Notable walled village**
- ■ **Ancestral halls of the five great clans**
- — **Present-day Hong Kong**

Family Pride

Each of Hong Kong's five great clans set up its own village and built an ancestral hall to show its family pride. Many of these ancestral halls are still standing. The Tang Ancestral Hall in Ping Shan is seven hundred years old and shows the success of the Tang clan. The Tangs can trace their ancestors back thirty generations in Hong Kong, and today's Tang clan has twenty-five thousand members.

The Arrival of Europeans

Early in the 1500s, European ships began arriving in the area. The region had several deep-water bays, which were needed for anchoring European ships. Trade began, but it was one-sided. The Chinese had silk, spices, and tea, which Europeans wanted. Europeans had nothing that interested the Chinese.

In the 1500s, the Portuguese became the first Europeans to arrive, and they quickly saw an opportunity to corner the Chinese goods trade. Through a mixture of diplomacy and bullying, the Portuguese established a trading center on the island of Macau, to the west of Hong Kong, in 1557. At the time, pirates

The Portuguese established a settlement in Macau in 1557. It was the first European settlement in China.

The Canton System

The Chinese viewed all Europeans as "barbarians." The Qianlong emperor banned all European ships, except those from Russia, from northern Chinese ports. This limited foreigners to trading under what became known as the Canton System, which lasted from 1757 to 1842. There were five rules of the Canton System:

1. Foreigners could not trade in Canton during the winter.
2. Foreigners visiting the city had to live in one of the thirteen Canton factories.
3. Chinese citizens could not work for or get money from the foreigners.
4. Chinese traders could not gain trading information about the international market from foreigners.
5. Foreign ships had to anchor in specific areas and be inspected by Chinese officials.

plagued the South China Sea, and the Portuguese helped control the pirates and the loss of goods to raiders. This improved the relationship between the Chinese and the Portuguese, but not enough to make China welcome the foreigners.

In 1672, the English East India Company secured a foothold in China and set up a trading post on the large island of Taiwan to the east of Hong Kong. The British were determined to trade with China, and the East India Company had a royal charter to push the Chinese into trade. East India Company ships made regular trips to the region, including to Canton, now known as Guangzhou, which lies about 75 miles (120 km) north of Hong Kong. It was in Guangzhou that an English base in China was founded.

Opium naturally occurs in poppy plants. Chinese opium traders had to boil the poppy pods to extract the drug so they could sell it.

Opium: The Stuff of Wars

While the British wanted Chinese tea, silk, spices, craft goods, metalwork, and art, the Chinese had no interest in wool, British steel, or anything else British. In 1773, to balance the trade situation, the British began selling a product to China that had been rare there before: opium.

England controlled much of the opium from India and the Middle East and brought it to China to trade. By 1790, Chinese citizens were so addicted to opium that traders were buying four thousand chests of opium a year. They traded valuable silver for addictive drugs. Emperor Jiaqing banned opium trade, but importers in Guangzhou and British traders would not give up such a moneymaker. Opium was better than money in Guangzhou. The British could get anything they wanted if they had opium to trade. A way around the ban was found: smuggling.

A British ship carrying opium would anchor several miles offshore. Small boats met the ship, and the opium was transferred to the boats. During the night, the opium would be rowed into port. When British ships arrived in port, they carried no banned goods.

Emperor Daoguang tried to limit the opium trade, but with little success.

Silver, silk, spices, and other goods flowed out of China, but in return, the opium that those goods brought did not build the economy. By 1830, the Chinese economy was in crisis. In 1839, Emperor Daoguang appointed an overseer to stop the opium trade. Soldiers marched into Guangzhou and laid siege to the factories where British opium dealers lived and worked. After six weeks of being deprived of food, the British handed over more than twenty thousand chests of opium.

The Chinese government mixed the opium with lime and poured it into a river. The British were not willing to give up such a lucrative trade. In 1839, the First Opium War began.

British ships blockaded southern China's ports. They fired on Chinese ships, progressed farther up the coast, and eventually captured Nanjing. After two years of British attacks, the Qing government gave in. They negotiated the Treaty of Nanjing with the British. The Chinese had to pay 20 million ounces (567 metric tons) of silver to the British, a quarter of it to compensate for the twenty thousand chests of opium destroyed in Guangzhou. They also opened five ports to British trade and gave up Hong Kong Island. The British now had a place to build a colony.

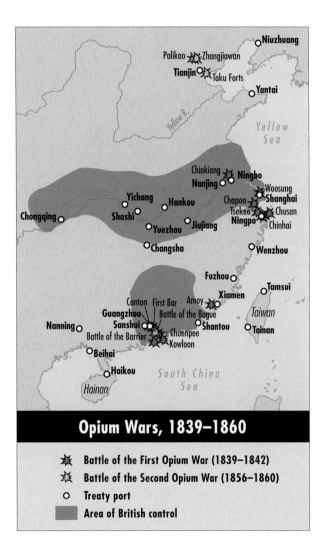

Opium Wars, 1839–1860

⚔ Battle of the First Opium War (1839–1842)
⚔ Battle of the Second Opium War (1856–1860)
○ Treaty port
▨ Area of British control

The New Colony

In 1842, the British moved into Hong Kong, a small, traditionally Chinese town of about 3,500 people. Building began immediately, with prime locations snapped up by the *hongs*, the trading companies located in Guangzhou and Macau. The navy set up a base on the waterfront, while the army established a post on the slopes of what became Victoria Peak. The site was first called Queen's Town and later renamed Victoria. Within three years, Hong Kong's population had increased to 25,000.

Almost immediately, British companies continued with the opium trade in China. The British also brought in their culture. The Happy Valley racetrack was built, establishing the first English-style racecourse in Asia. Most British followed the Anglican church, and the British built St. John's Cathedral as a religious center. In 1855, the construction of Government House was completed, providing a site for legal and government activities.

When the Chinese had signed the Treaty of Nanjing in 1842, they had expected the opium trade to stop. The British companies continued to press, though, trying to expand their trade in opium and other goods deeper into China and into more ports. At the same time, piracy became widespread in the South China Sea. The search for pirates gave Chinese officials a reason to stop and search ships. In 1856, the Chinese

In the mid-1800s, Victoria quickly became a thriving English city.

stopped the *Arrow*, a ship that was owned by the Chinese but flew a British flag. The *Arrow* became the reason behind yet another war, the Arrow War, or the Second Opium War.

By 1857, opium imports had reached seventy thousand chests a year. At this point, China, European nations, and the United States were all unhappy with the Treaty of Nanjing. Britain was making too much money from opium. Other nations wanted to trade with China. China wanted Western nations to leave it alone. The Chinese did not like the way Western customs affected Chinese traditions.

The Second Opium War took place between 1856 and 1858. It was not really about the opium but rather about opening China to Western trade. The Chinese signed a treaty with the British and French in 1858, although it would take another two years before peace was official. The Chinese resented having foreign embassies in their capital, Beijing. The British and French used their joint military power to attack Chinese coastal forts. In the end, the Chinese signed the trade agreements, but they remained angry over being forced to open their country to the foreigners.

The British were uncomfortable with China being so close to its colony in Hong Kong. This concern led British officials to add Kowloon to the British colony as a condition for peace after the Second Opium War. In 1898, the British forced China to sign a lease renting the New Territories and outlying islands to the British. The lease would run for ninety-nine years, ending in 1997. Britain would eventually have to give the territory back to the Chinese.

Chinese fighters burn British warehouses during the Second Opium War.

The Twentieth Century

Between 1900 and 1940, Hong Kong grew in financial importance and population. In 1911, a revolution in China overthrew the Qing emperor and his government. The Republic of China was founded in 1912. In the years that followed, unrest continued as Chinese nationalism grew, sometimes seeping into Hong Kong.

In 1937, the Japanese invaded eastern China. Under the onslaught of the Japanese army, thousands of Chinese fled to the south. Within a year, the Japanese controlled most of China. Refugees poured into Hong Kong, increasing the population to 1.5 million.

When World War II began in 1939, Japan became an ally of Germany, which had invaded many of its neighboring European nations. In 1941, Japan attacked Pearl Harbor, Hawaii, bringing the United States into World War II. Within hours of that attack, Japan also attacked Hong Kong. The British and their Hong Kong Chinese, Australian, and Canadian allies fought fiercely in the Battle of Hong Kong. Still, less than three weeks after Pearl Harbor, Allied forces were forced to give up control of Hong Kong.

Japanese soldiers sail into Hong Kong on December 25, 1941, following the colony's surrender.

More than one million Chinese people fled to Hong Kong in the early 1950s, escaping the communist government in mainland China.

Allies finally defeated Japan and Germany in 1945. The end of World War II signaled a new era in Hong Kong. In East Asia, Hong Kong grew wealthier. It became a financial power and a tourist destination very different from the rest of China.

By 1949, at the end of a civil war, China had become a communist nation under the rule of Mao Zedong. Communism is the opposite of capitalism. In theory, communists share wealth for the greater good of all people. Capitalists make money and keep it for their own good. In Mao's China, religion was looked down upon and sometimes suppressed. All private property was confiscated. All enterprises came to be owned by the state. People who spoke out against Mao or communism were sent to work camps to correct their mistaken beliefs. The people of Hong Kong did

The Japanese captured many British, Canadian, and Australian troops during the Battle of Hong Kong in 1941. Most of these soldiers were transferred to prisoner of war camps in Kowloon. The Japanese also captured about three thousand non-Chinese civilians who had been living in Hong Kong. For the next three and a half years, those men, women, and children were held in the Stanley Internment Camp in Hong Kong. Food and medical facilities were poor. Many prisoners suffered from disease and malnutrition. Adults organized work duties, arranged a school, and planned plays and musicals for entertainment. The people lived out the rest of the war in this internment camp and were not freed until the day after the Japanese surrendered.

not want to live under the rigid Chinese government. Mao was content to let the British rule Hong Kong. He considered Hong Kong a window to the world for China, which was isolated from the Western world until the 1970s. When Mao died in 1976, Deng Xiaoping became China's supreme leader. Deng was determined to take over Hong Kong when the lease with Britain ran out in 1997.

Into the HKSAR

Great Britain and China began negotiations for the handover of Hong Kong in the 1980s. British prime minister Margaret Thatcher visited Beijing, the capital of China, to discuss what would happen to Hong Kong after Britain relinquished control of it. The talks were bitter and angry. Finally, the two nations agreed on a Joint Declaration in 1984. Under this declaration, Hong Kong would be treated differently from the rest of China for fifty years after the turnover. Hong Kong would be known as the Hong Kong Special Administrative Region (HKSAR). HKSAR would keep its capitalist economy and exercise local autonomy under a democratizing local government.

Not everyone believed the handover would go smoothly. During the 1990s, many of Hong Kong's best-educated and most successful people moved to Canada and Australia. This loss of talent was called the Brain Drain. Hong Kongers remained tense waiting to see what would happen. The turnover took place on June 30, 1997. British rule had come to an end.

Chinese leader Deng Xiaoping and British prime minister Margaret Thatcher meet to discuss the transfer of Hong Kong to Chinese control.

The first decades of the HKSAR have been a bit rocky. The Chinese and Hong Kongers do not always agree on the best policies for the SAR. On many topics, Hong Kongers are divided. Many are pro-China, but an even larger number are pro-democracy. Because of pressure for greater democracy, in 2012 Hong Kong officials increased the size of the Legislative Council to seventy.

In 2014, the vast majority of Hong Kongers favored citizens having a greater voice in selecting candidates for chief executive. They wanted the people of Hong Kong to be able to nominate candidates, but Beijing politicians refused, instead announcing that a nominating committee would select the candidates. In September 2014, protesters flooded the streets in a massive pro-democracy rally. Some protesters moved in to

The SAR Chief Executive

In 1997, the Chinese chose a multimillionaire shipping tycoon named Tung Chee-hwa (1937–) to be the first SAR chief executive, the head of Hong Kong's government. Almost immediately, a financial crisis hit Asia, including Hong Kong. Tung's plans to focus on housing, education, and the elderly were pushed aside as he desperately tried to save Hong Kong's sinking economy. In 2002, he was elected to a second term, but Hong Kongers were dissatisfied with his leadership. Hundreds of thousands of Hong Kongers took to the streets to demand his resignation and protest his government's attempt to pass a law that would restrict freedom of speech in Hong Kong. In 2005, Tung Chee-hwa finally resigned.

occupy Admiralty, the central administrative region in Hong Kong, bringing tents and barricades. Others occupied the busy roads in Mongkok, on the Kowloon side. The protest was well organized and polite, but the police responded with tear gas and pepper spray. In the months that followed, there were arrests and clashes as the police tried to clear the protesters. The protests became less common after the end of that year.

The relationship between Hong Kong and China remains an uneasy one. China wants more control over the SAR. Hong Kong wants a democratically elected government and economic freedom. How this situation will be resolved remains unclear.

Protesters repeatedly filled the streets of Hong Kong in 2014, demanding a greater say in the way the region is run.

CHAPTER 5

One Country, Two Systems

THE AGREEMENT BETWEEN GREAT BRITAIN AND CHINA called for "one country, two systems," meaning that Hong Kong would be ruled differently than the rest of China. Although this is the official policy, it has not been easy to make it happen. Chinese officials want greater control over Hong Kong's government. Hong Kong wants to move forward toward open elections and a greater say in SAR laws and policies, as the Joint Declaration promised. The two sides remain at a standoff.

Opposite: **Election workers prepare to count ballots at a polling station in Hong Kong.**

Hong Kong's Basic Law

Hong Kong does not have a constitution. Instead, it has the Basic Law, a blueprint for how Hong Kong will be governed from 1997 to 2047.

The Basic Law calls for three branches of government: executive, legislative, and judiciary. It also states that Hong Kong residents can own property, vote in elections, run for office, practice choice of religion, marry whomever they wish, and form and join trade unions. Any changes to the Basic Law, however, are

HONG KONG, CHINA

Leung Chun-ying, the chief executive of Hong Kong, is considered to have a close relationship with the Chinese government in Beijing.

made by the People's Republic of China. This means that while Hong Kongers are granted specific freedoms, the Chinese government can change the Basic Law as it chooses. The Chinese can take away any freedoms that they have given.

The Executive Council

The head of Hong Kong's government is called the chief executive, but the true head of state is the president of China. An election committee made up of 1,200 representatives elects the chief executive, who serves for a five-year period. Leung Chun-ying was elected to this position in 2012. The chief executive suggests laws, signs bills and budgets, and makes decisions on government policy.

The chief executive appoints the members of the Executive Council, selecting from among important Hong Kong officials, members of the Legislative Council, and members of the public. There are fifteen official and fourteen unofficial Executive Council members. Each oversees an area such as finance, education, justice, and security. All Executive Council members serve for the same period as the chief executive.

Hong Kong's Government

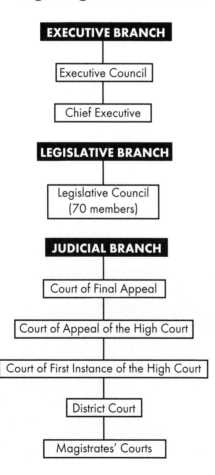

EXECUTIVE BRANCH

Executive Council

Chief Executive

LEGISLATIVE BRANCH

Legislative Council
(70 members)

JUDICIAL BRANCH

Court of Final Appeal

Court of Appeal of the High Court

Court of First Instance of the High Court

District Court

Magistrates' Courts

The Legislative Branch

The Legislative Council is a seventy-member body responsible for making, changing, or repealing laws in Hong Kong. It also debates public issues and examines and approves budgets. The councillors approve the appointment of judges to the Court of Final Appeal, as well as the appointment of the Chief Judge of the High Court. Councillors must also approve taxes and government expenses.

Thirty-five members of the Legislative Council are elected by the people by geographical constituencies, or election districts. The other thirty-five members are elected by functional

A speech by the Hong Kong financial chief is broadcast on a large screen in the Legislative Council.

Hong Kong's National Anthem

Because Hong Kong is an administrative region of China, the country uses the Chinese national anthem, "Yiyongjun Jinxingqu" ("March of the Volunteers"). The lyrics were written by poet Tian Han, and the music is the work of composer Nie Er. The song honors those who fought against the Japanese invasion in the 1930s. It was adopted as the official anthem in 1982.

English translation

Arise! All those who refuse to be slaves!
Let our flesh and blood forge our new Great Wall!
The Chinese nation has arrived at its most perilous time.
Every person is forced to expel his very last roar.
Arise! Arise! Arise!
One million hearts beating as one,
Brave the enemy's fire, March on!
Brave the enemy's fire, March on!
March on! March on! On!

constituencies. A functional constituency is a professional or special interest group that may be concerned with teaching, law, social welfare, medicine, finance, industry, commercial ventures, labor, and architecture or land surveying. There is also a rural constituency.

The Judicial Branch

Hong Kong's judiciary is a mix of British and Chinese tradition. As in Great Britain, judges and lawyers in Hong Kong's high courts wear wigs and robes. Trials and hearings are held in English and Chinese. There are three high courts: the Court of Final Appeal, the Court of Appeal of the High Court, and the Court of First Instance of the High Court. In addi-

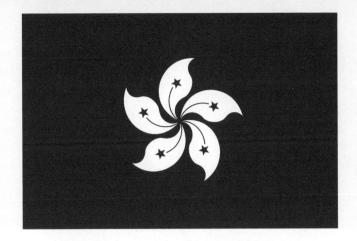

Hong Kong's Flag

The flag of Hong Kong is a white bauhinia orchid against a red background. The flower includes five petals, each with a star in its center. The five stars link Hong Kong's flag to the Chinese flag, which also includes five stars. Both flags use the same shade of red, which represents happiness and communism. The bauhinia orchid is the national flower of Hong Kong.

tion, Hong Kong also has a District Court, seven Magistrates' Courts, and other more specific courts such as juvenile courts, which handle cases involving young people.

The three high courts are the main criminal courts. The Court of Final Appeal, which has five judges, hears appeals of cases that have been ruled upon in lower courts and deal with an issue of the Basic Law. The Court of Appeal of the High Court hears appeals from the Court of First Instance and the District Court.

The Court of First Instance hears a wide range of cases, such as the ending of a corporation or the adoption of a child. This court also deals with criminal cases such as murder or robbery. The cases are heard before a judge and a jury of either seven or nine citizens.

The District Court was first established in 1953 during British rule. The District Court can handle legal matters with claims of up to about US$130,000 (1 million Hong Kong dollars) and criminal cases that might impose prison sentences of less than seven years. Magistrates' Courts handle minor criminal cases.

Tai chi exercise classes are common in districts throughout the region.

District Governments

Hong Kong is divided into eighteen districts, each of which has a district council that promotes recreation, culture, and community events, such as parades, fairs, or sporting events. The councils also advise the central government about matters that are important to the people in their districts. In addition, district councils investigate the quality of local facilities, the environment in their districts, and the health and welfare of citizens.

The Center of Hong Kong Government

The city of Victoria served as the capital of the British colony of Hong Kong from 1842 until 1997. Although it is no longer an official capital, the government offices are still located there. The city, now usually called Central, is located on the northern shore of Hong Kong Island. It is a city of skyscrapers. Some are office buildings, while others are apartments. Most of the city's nearly one million residents live in high rises. A maze of elevated walkways and tunnels connects the buildings, so for many people it is possible to get from home to work to shopping without ever touching the ground.

Central is the main business area in the Hong Kong region. It is a major world banking capital, and many companies have their headquarters there.

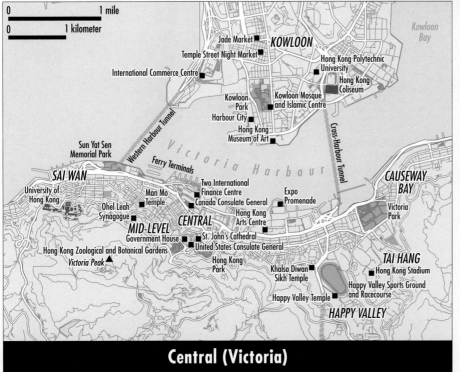

Central (Victoria)

Victoria Harbour, which separates Hong Kong Island from Kowloon, is the site of the Hong Kong region's largest port. It is one of the busiest in the world.

People who want to escape Central's skyscraper canyons take a tram to the top of Victoria Peak, which looms just behind the city. From there, they can enjoy a spectacular view of the towering buildings and Victoria Harbour.

CHAPTER 6

On the Job

A LETTER CAME FROM THE UNIVERSITY OF HONG Kong School of Economics and Finance. Wong Chee-ying has been accepted to the program to get a master's degree in finance. He has just finished a college degree in economics while working mornings in the Hong Kong Stock Exchange. In two years, he will have his degree and get a big promotion.

Wong is twenty-four and a wizard with modeling and forecasting stock changes. He will be joining the growing number of Hong Kong's working population in the financial services industry. Wong loves the excitement and pressure of the stock market. When one of his stock picks produces a huge profit for investors, his reputation as a financial genius increases. By the time he has his master's degree, he'll have a long list of clients using his stock-selecting advice.

Opposite: **Businesspeople walk past the Hong Kong Stock Exchange. Finance, real estate, and insurance employ about 20 percent of all workers in the SAR.**

Hong Kong's Service Industries (2013)	
Service Sector	**% of Economy**
Import/export, wholesale and retail trades	24.9
Public administration, social and personal services	17.1
Financing and insurance	16.3
Real estate, professional and business services	11.1
Ownership of premises	10.4
Transportation, storage, postal and courier services	5.9
Information and communications	3.6
Accommodation and food services	3.5
Total of service sectors	92.8

Hong Kong's Service Industry

Hong Kong's economy is not like that of most countries. It has some agriculture, but so little that more than 95 percent of food is imported. There is no mining worth mentioning. Manufacturing accounts for only about 1.4 percent of the

Hong Kong's Richest Man

Li Ka-shing is Hong Kong's wealthiest citizen. Called one of the world's great empire builders by *Forbes* magazine, Li commands an extensive corporation that operates in fifty-two countries and has 270,000 employees. As a boy of fourteen, Li quit school and became an apprentice in a leather watchband factory. At fourteen, he worked for a plastics company. He began his own business in 1950, making plastic toys and household goods. From this modest beginning, Li built a powerful company, Cheung Kong Holdings, that deals with property, financial investments, life sciences, and technology. Today, Li is worth about US$32 billion.

Workers labor high atop a new skyscraper in Central.

SAR's economy, and construction another 4 percent. That leaves more than 90 percent of the economy unaccounted for, and that percentage is taken up by service industries. Services include all aspects of banking and finance, tourism, and retail sales. Importing and exporting are also services.

Hong Kong is one of the top international financial centers in the world. Seventy of the world's top one hundred banks have offices in Hong Kong. Hong Kong's stock exchange is the sixth largest in the world, and second only to the Tokyo Stock Exchange in Asia. Hong Kong also plays a leading role in the insurance industry.

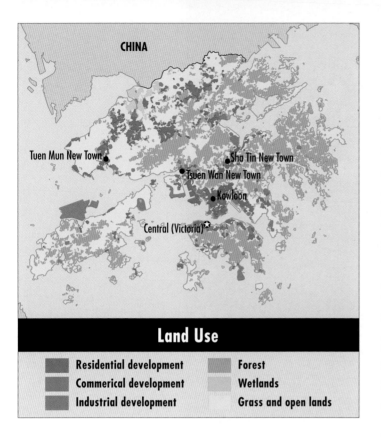

CHINA

Tuen Mun New Town

Sha Tin New Town

Tsuen Wan New Town

Kowloon

Central (Victoria)

Land Use

Residential development
Commerical development
Industrial development

Forest
Wetlands
Grass and open lands

About 250,000 Hong Kongers work in the tourism industry. This industry includes everything from hotels to restaurants, and dolphin tours to Hong Kong's Disneyland. In 2013, 54.3 million tourists, most from mainland China, arrived in Hong Kong. The government provides a Mega Events Fund to help non-profit groups supersize parades or cultural presentations into blockbuster, tourist-generating events. This program has been successful, as every holiday, millions of Chinese cross the border for a vacation in Hong Kong.

Manufacturing and Agriculture

Manufacturing makes up only 1.4 percent of Hong Kong's economy. Hong Kong has a thriving industry in jewelry, gold, and silver goods. Hong Kong also produces plastics, electrical machinery and parts, and medicines. These products are exported mainly to China, with some going to the United States, Singapore, Taiwan, Vietnam, and Switzerland.

In Hong Kong, agriculture accounts for only 0.1 percent of the economy. Land is expensive, and only 1,739 acres (704 ha) of land are farmed in the entire region. The SAR's main crops include Chinese white cabbage, flowering cabbage, let-

tuce, kale, leaf mustard, spring onions, and chives. Winter crops, such as spinach and watercress, appear in street markets when the weather is cold by Hong Kong standards. Some

A worker in Hong Kong carefully adjusts stones while making jewelry.

What Hong Kong Grows and Makes

AGRICULTURE (2008)

Vegetables	16,400 metric tons
Chickens	4,664,000 animals
Pigs	87,240 animals

MANUFACTURING (PERCENTAGE OF EXPORTS, 2013)

Jewelry, gold, and silver goods	15.6%
Plastics	11.3%
Electrical machinery and parts	5%

Although vegetables grow well in the region, land is valuable and is often used for building instead.

crops, such as sweet peppers, cauliflower, carrots, and celery, are also available mostly in winter. Small amounts of citrus fruits, lychee, longan, guava, and papaya are grown in the foothills of Hong Kong's mountains.

The SAR has a total of forty-three pig farms and even fewer poultry farms. There is one licensed dairy farm. Most meat, cheese, butter, and milk is imported from China, Australia, and New Zealand.

The SAR is surrounded by water, and more than two hundred species of edible fish live in those waters. Fishing and aquaculture (fish farming) provide about 30 percent of seafood eaten by Hong Kongers. Fishers bring in hairtail, mackerel, scad, bigeye, pomfret, and croaker. Smaller fishing operations also catch shrimp, sea cucumber, sea slugs, and turtles. While this bounty from the sea is great, many species are being overfished. The Hong Kong government has to control the management of fisheries or there will be no fish left to catch.

Aquaculture is beginning to have an impact on Hong Kong fish markets. Most aquaculture operations are located in the northwest sector of the New Territories. Most fish farms raise carp, tilapia, or gray mullet.

Making a Living

In recent years, the unemployment rate has been low, often about 3 percent. That means that most Hong Kongers looking

Money Facts

Hong Kong's currency is the Hong Kong dollar, which is divided into one hundred cents. Hong Kong dollar notes circulate in $10, $20, $50, $100, $500, and $1,000 denominations. Coins come in 10¢, 20¢, 50¢, $1, $2, $5, and $10. In 2015, $1HK equaled US$0.13, and US$1.00 equaled $7.75HK.

Three different banks print Hong Kong currency, and each bank's notes look slightly different from the others. A $1,000HK note from the Hong Kong and Shanghai Banking Corporation (HSBC) is brown and features a lion's head on the front and a scene of the Dragon Boat Festival on the back. The note of the Bank of China (Hong Kong) is orange and has an orchid and a high-rise building on the front and a scene of Hong Kong's main harbor on the back. The Standard Chartered Bank's version of the note is yellow with brown and orange. It features a dragon on the front and a symbol of heritage and technology on the back. Regardless of the bank, each denomination has a color scheme. Notes of $500HK are brownish, while the $100HK notes are mostly red. Fifty-dollar notes are green, and $20HK notes are blue.

Weights and Measures

Hong Kong uses three different systems of measure: the Chinese Qing system, the British imperial system, and the metric system. Retail businesses such as butcher shops or vegetable sellers can use whichever of the three systems suits them best.

	Chinese Qing	British Imperial	Metric
Length	li, tcek, tsun	miles, feet, inches	meters, centimeters
Weight	jin, catty, tael	pounds, ounces	kilograms, grams
Precious metals	tael, mace, candareen	troy ounces, troy drams	grams, milligrams

for jobs can find them. However, many jobs in Hong Kong pay poorly. The gap between the wealthy and the poor in Hong Kong is the widest of anywhere in the world. Minimum wage jobs, such as working in a fast-food restaurant or cleaning houses, pay only $32.50HK (US$4.19) per hour, far less than the United States' minimum wage. The average worker in Hong Kong finds it difficult to afford housing and food.

In recent years, average wages have increased in Hong Kong by about 30 percent, but housing costs have more than doubled. Buying even the smallest apartment is beyond the reach of an average family. Groceries are affordable for people who purchase from open markets and buy the basics only: rice, fruit and vegetables, and a small amount of protein. Eating out, even at a fast-food restaurant, costs the equivalent of more than an hours' labor after taxes are taken out. A night out at the movies (complete with soda, popcorn, and a hot dog) runs $80HK (US$10.32) a person, or about two hours' worth of after-tax minimum wages. Hong Kong may be a world finance center, but for the average family, it is expensive.

Transportation

Hong Kong has an extensive public transportation system. People get around by bus, train, the mass transit rail, light-rail, and ferries. For those with more spending money, there are taxicabs in all major business centers. For those with less money, there is always walking.

Buses run from 6:00 a.m. to midnight every day of the week. Nearly every city block has a bus stop, and buses are clearly marked by destination in English and Chinese.

Hong Kong is densely populated, and the subway is often crowded.

Hong Kong has more double-decker trams than any other place in the world.

Hong Kong Island has a tram service, which is similar to the bus system. Trams are double-decker–style and connect major hubs on the north shore of the island. The system is more than 110 years old, but it remains the main way to get around the Central district on the island. Called the "ding-

The Octopus Card

Few people in Hong Kong carry small change. Instead, they use an Octopus card. The Octopus card can be used on all forms of public transportation and at the movies, stores and supermarkets, hospitals, schools, public service locations, and sports facilities. The card can also be used for online shopping, traveling throughout Hong Kong, or paying bills.

Hong Kongers can reload their Octopus cards with cash at most fast-food restaurants. There are special Octopus cards for senior citizens and children, which are preloaded with age-related discounts for certain types of transportation.

ding" because of the bells that warn traffic that the tram is coming, the trams are slow, packed, and cheap. They cost only $2.30HK (US$0.30) for adults.

Hong Kong also has a mass transit railway and rail lines that connect Hong Kong Island, Lantau, Kowloon, and the New Town cities in the New Territories. Hong Kong has a light-rail that runs on electricity. The light-rail connects New Territories towns in the western districts.

Roads and underwater tunnels connect Kowloon to Hong Kong Island or Lantau. There are also ferries that connect the major cities to the outlying islands.

A ferry boat carries passengers across Victoria Harbour. It takes just eight to ten minutes for the boat to cross the harbor.

CHAPTER 7

A Growing Region

THE VAST MAJORITY OF HONG KONGERS ARE CHINESE, but Hong Kong Chinese do not always feel connected to mainlanders. Most Hong Kongers speak Cantonese Chinese, follow Chinese customs, eat Chinese food, and keep Chinese traditions, but they have their own identity, separate from that of the mainland Chinese.

Opposite: **Pedestrians fill a street in Hong Kong, one of the most densely populated places in the world.**

The SAR Population

About 93 percent of Hong Kongers are Chinese, 2 percent are Indonesian, and another 2 percent are Filipino. The remaining 3 percent have a variety of backgrounds, including British, Indian, Australian, Pakistani, and Portuguese. The British, Indians, and Portuguese have been in Hong Kong for more than 150 years. During that time, many have married Chinese spouses and consider themselves Hong Kongers.

Ethnic Hong Kong (2012)	
Chinese	93%
Indonesian	2%
Filipino	2%
Others (including British, Australian, Indian, Canadian, Portuguese, Pakistani, Nepalese, Japanese, Thai)	3%

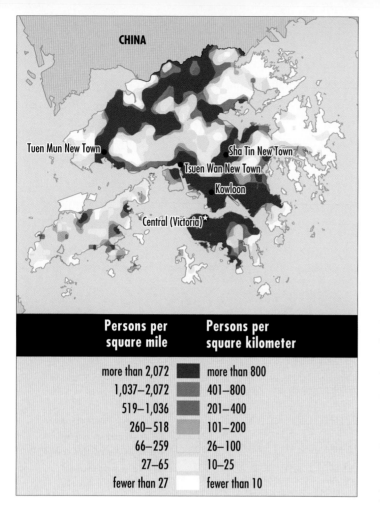

Persons per square mile		Persons per square kilometer
more than 2,072		more than 800
1,037–2,072		401–800
519–1,036		201–400
260–518		101–200
66–259		26–100
27–65		10–25
fewer than 27		fewer than 10

Hong Kong contains a tightly packed population of more than seven million people. Although the density of all of Hong in 2014 was 17,024 people per square mile (6,575 per sq km), about 70 percent of the land in Hong Kong cannot be used for housing, so the people of Hong Kong are in fact packed into a much smaller area. Never is the actual population density clearer than at lunchtime on a weekday when crowds jostle to grab lunch from a noodle shop or fast-food restaurant.

To accommodate all these people, the government is creating more housing by building New Towns that mainly serve as bedroom communities for workers. It is building hundreds of thousands of housing units, mostly apartments in high-rise buildings.

Population of Major Urban Areas (2011)

Kowloon	2,108,419
Central (Victoria)	992,221
Tsuen Wan New Town	801,800
Sha Tin New Town	630,000
Tuen Mun New Town	470,900

Going to School

The SAR government provides every child with twelve years of free education. Many parents, however, choose to send their children to private school. Hong Kong has fifteen schools run by the English Schools Foundation, offering classes in English. Other international schools also teach non-Chinese speaking students.

The first level of education is for kindergartners ages three to five. Many kindergartens are located in high-rise apartment units.

Primary school is for six years and covers children ages six through twelve. Students learn Chinese, math, English as a second language, science, and history. Because schools are crowded, many Hong Kong schools have shifts. There is a morning session and an afternoon session, and students also attend class on Saturdays.

On average, primary school classes in Hong Kong have twenty-seven students.

Born in Hong Kong

Li Chao-xing and her husband are on the way to Hong Kong, and they are in a bit of a hurry. Chao-xing is pregnant, but she does not want to give birth in Guangdong in southern China. Like many other Chinese women, she wants to have her baby in Hong Kong.

There are many reasons women from the Chinese mainland head to Hong Kong to give birth. The quality of medical care in Hong Kong is superior to what is available in Guangdong. A Chinese baby born in Hong Kong has the right to live there and have all the benefits of Hong Kong life. A child receives twelve years of free public education, which is also better than the education children receive in mainland China.

In 2012, four out of ten babies born in Hong Kong were born to Chinese mainlanders. For a while, Hong Kong hospitals believed attracting mothers-to-be was a good idea. Hospitals filled empty beds, and mainland families spent plenty of money while the mother and her baby were in the hospital.

But in recent years, the government has begun to see the baby boom as a problem. When the child reaches school age, the parents typically remain in mainland China and pay taxes there. The children live with other relatives in Hong Kong during their school years. The government provides an education and other services, even though the child's parents pay no Hong Kong taxes. The Hong Kong government now believes this is too expensive, but efforts to stop the flow of pregnant women into Hong Kong are having mixed success.

What's for Lunch?

School lunch in Hong Kong consists of portions that are a third rice, pasta, or noodles; a third vegetables; a sixth meat, and a sixth fruit. Students are taught to "eat smart," which means balancing nutrition and avoiding empty calories. A typical lunch might be buckwheat noodles, low-fat yogurt, steamed carrots and broccoli, a small portion of roast pork or chicken, and low-fat milk.

Secondary education also covers six years and is similar to American middle school and high school. Secondary grades, called forms, are numbered 1 to 5. Some schools also have form 6.

Secondary school students head home after school.

Days can be long for secondary school students in Hong Kong. An average teenager is up before 6:00 a.m., has a quick breakfast, and runs to catch the public bus or tram. If teens have after-school activities, such as sports or drama, it is likely that they will not be home until 7:00 p.m. Then, there is dinner and homework.

At the end of secondary school, all students take an examination, called the Hong Kong Diploma of Secondary Education Examination. In an effort to get a good grade on the final exam, many students attend cram schools. These are after-school or nightly courses to help students get high scores. Since place-

Badminton is a popular sport in Hong Kong schools.

Students in Hong Kong have no trouble deciding what to wear to school. All schools have a specific uniform, and all students are expected to wear their uniforms every day. Many of the uniforms are based on British styles. Some look like sailor suits. Others are plain tops and trousers. Girls wear skirts or dresses. Primary school boys wear shorts, usually gray or blue. School uniforms include blazers, and most have badges to indicate the school. In the winter, students wear sweaters. Shirts are white or blue and also have an embroidered badge. Summer uniforms are white cotton trousers, skirts, or shorts, along with white socks and white or blue shirts.

ment in a good Hong Kong university depends on the exam scores, families make sacrifices to pay for cram school.

The SAR has nineteen colleges and universities where students can earn degrees in a full range of subjects. Students with degrees go on to work in Hong Kong or leave the SAR in search of jobs in other countries. Since all students who graduate secondary school can read, write, and speak both Chinese and English, they are sought after for job placements.

In addition to academic subjects, the SAR's education plan provides vocational education. Vocational schools train carpenters, electricians, and plumbers. They educate chefs so they can work in one of the SAR's hundreds of restaurants. Students can pursue careers in computer technology and repair through SAR vocational schools. Trade skills pay well, and students must work hard to get a certificate showing their knowledge.

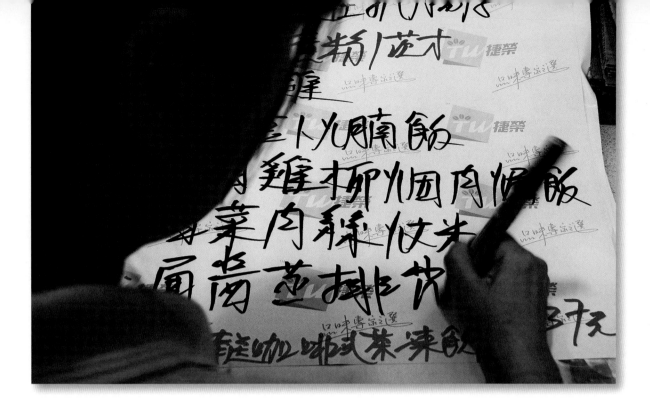

In Mainland China, many Chinese characters have been simplified so that they use fewer lines. In Hong Kong, however, the traditional characters, as shown here, are used.

Languages

The Chinese language does not have an alphabet. Instead, it uses characters, with each character standing for a simple word. To read a newspaper, a person must know about three thousand characters. There are many different versions, or dialects, of spoken Chinese, but they all use the same characters. This means that the written language stays the same, but the sounds that go along with each character vary from one dialect to the next.

Most people in Hong Kong speak Cantonese Chinese. Many others speak Hakka (from Han Chinese), Chiu Chow, Hokkien, or Shanghainese. About 46 percent of the people in Hong Kong also speak English. Chinese is the language spoken in the home. English is preferred for government, business, and tourism.

Street names are a mix of English and Chinese: Lai Chi Kok Road in Kowloon intersects with Prince Edward Road and Argyle Street. Signs for buses, markets, trains, and food products are printed in both English and Chinese. Either language may be used during an arrest or a trial, and sometimes both are used in these instances. In restaurants, menus are often printed in both languages, but when language fails, people just point to what they want. That works fine for both the diner and the cook.

Signs in the airport are in both Chinese and English.

CHAPTER 8

Following a Faith

CHUI BO-JING WAS BORN INTO A BUDDHIST FAMILY in Hong Kong. At age sixteen, he decided that a life dedicated to following Buddha's path to enlightenment would suit him. He joined the Po Lin Monastery on Lantau Island. Although he knew much about Buddhism, life in the monastery was very different from his life at home. He spent many hours each day in prayer and meditation and was given a teacher to be his guide to life as a monk.

Now, three years later, Chui Bo-jing is ready to be ordained as a monk. His head is shaved, and he is given his Buddhist name. Chui will spend his life trying to gain enlightenment through the example of the Buddha. He must open his heart to the spiritual teachings of Buddha. He feels at peace. He belongs to the Po Lin community, and Po Lin belongs to him.

Opposite: **The massive Tian Tan Buddha, on Lantau Island, is one of the largest bronze Buddhas in the world.**

Religion in Hong Kong (2010)	
Buddhist	21.3%
Daoist	14.2%
Christian	11.8%
Muslim	3.0%
Other	49.7%

Buddhism

Buddhism is the most common religion in Hong Kong. Hong Kong has more than one million Buddhists. Buddhists believe that people are reincarnated, or that their soul is born again. They believe that what they do in this life affects what their next life will be like. Buddhism teaches that by letting go of desire, people can avoid suffering. They eventually achieve nirvana, or enlightenment, which ends the cycle of death and rebirth.

Buddhist monks gather at a monastery to pray.

Lanterns and incense
fill a Daoist temple in
Hong Kong.

Daily prayer and community service are important to Buddhists. Followers of Buddhism pray at temples and at home. The Hong Kong Buddhist community supports social services for the poor, sick, and elderly.

Daoism

Daoism has a two-thousand-year history in China. Daoists believe in living a simple life that is in harmony with nature. Different branches of Daoism believe in different deities. Two important deities for Hong Kong Daoists are Laozi, also called Tai Shang Lao Jun, and Tin Hau. Laozi, who lived in the sixth century BCE, was Daoism's first philosopher. Tin Hau is honored as the Goddess of the Sea. Since Hong Kong has long been a seafaring community, sailors and fishers ask Tin Hau's blessing for a safe voyage and a good catch.

Confucius taught people to be respectful and loyal toward parents, bosses, and elders. He also taught them to be kind toward people in lower positions.

There are more than three hundred Daoist temples in Hong Kong. Among the most popular are the Wong Tai Sin Temple in Kowloon, the Man Mo Temple in Sheung Wan, and the Che Kung Temple in Sha Tin. Hong Kong is home to more than one million Daoists.

Confucianism

Confucianism is as much a philosophy as a religion. It began with Confucius (551–479 BCE), a philosopher and teacher who was known for following a moral code of behavior. Confucius believed in the importance of honoring one's elders and educating the mind. The followers of Confucius have a strong belief in the value of education. Today, Confucians run a number of schools in Hong Kong. Every year, they hold a major festival honoring Confucius on his birthday.

Christianity

Both Roman Catholic and Protestant churches have established communities in Hong Kong. Roman Catholicism has been in Hong Kong since the region became British territory. Today, there are about 375,000 Catholics in the SAR. Most masses are conducted in Chinese, although there are English and Tagalog (Filipino) services in the city. Catholic parishes support schools, kindergartens, and daycare centers. There are also Catholic hospitals, homes for senior citizens, and recreation centers.

An Anglican church in Wan Chai, Hong Kong, combines elements of Western and Chinese architecture. Anglicanism is one of the largest Protestant denominations in Hong Kong.

Religious Holidays

Lunar New Year	January or February
Ching Ming Festival	Early April
Good Friday	March or April
Easter Saturday	March or April
Easter Sunday	March or April
Dragon Boat Festival	June
Mid-Autumn Festival	September
Chung Yeung	October
Christmas	December 25

Protestantism in Hong Kong also dates back to the arrival of the British. Today, the region's 480,000 Protestants belong to many different denominations, or groups, including Anglican, Baptist, Lutheran, and many others. The Salvation Army has a large following, and its members are active in social welfare. Protestant churches also run schools, daycare centers, and social centers. Hong Kong has several Christian bookstores, and two weekly newspapers, the *Christian Weekly* and the *Christian Times*.

Other Religions

Many people in Hong Kong follow other faiths. There are sizable Muslim, Hindu, Sikh, and Jewish communities in the region. The Kowloon Mosque and Islamic Center, built in 1984, is one of five mosques in Hong Kong. The mosque includes prayer halls for men and women, a medical clinic, and a library.

Forty thousand of Hong Kong's Hindus meet in the Happy Valley Temple. The temple is a center for meditation, social

occasions, and religious festivals. Services, Hindu music, yoga classes, and communal meals provide a social center for many Hindus on Hong Kong Island.

When the British colonized Hong Kong, a number of Sikhs came from India to serve as police officers. Sikh soldiers in the British army built the first Sikh temple on Hong Kong Island in 1901. Today, the Khalsa Diwan Sikh Temple is the center of Sikh social life for ten thousand Sikhs. Khalsa Diwan provides free meals and housing for travelers, regardless of their religious beliefs.

The region's first synagogue, a Jewish house of worship, was completed in 1902. Three brothers named Sassoon, who belonged to a prominent Jewish family that settled in Hong Kong, donated the land for the Ohel Leah Synagogue. The synagogue remains a center of Hong Kong Jewish life today.

Some Muslim women, such as these teenagers in Kowloon, choose to completely cover their hair as a symbol of modesty.

CHAPTER 9

From Cricket to Cantopop

MANY SPORTS POPULAR IN HONG KONG ARE traditionally British. These include equestrian events, cricket, horse racing, squash, badminton, and rugby. The top equestrian event is the Hong Kong Masters, held yearly for the world's top twenty-five riders. This elite event features dressage, in which the horse must complete a series of precise movements, and jumping. The winner earns US$700,000.

Opposite: **A cricket player swings at the ball during the Hong Kong Cricket Sixes tournament.**

Sports of All Sorts

Cricket is extremely popular in Great Britain and former British colonies around the world, including Hong Kong. Like baseball, cricket uses a ball and a bat, but that's where the similarity ends. Bases are called wickets, and there are only two of them. Pitchers are bowlers, and they hurl the ball, bouncing it on the lawn before it reaches the batter. Runs can be made up to six at a time but only on a great hit. The Hong Kong Cricket Sixes tournament presents a fast, furious, and feverish

Hong Kong Horse Racing

Throughout the year, spectators flock to the Happy Valley Racecourse or the Sha Tin Racecourse for horse racing. Racing has been a Hong Kong sporting tradition since 1841. Today, jockeys and horses come from throughout the world to race in the Hong Kong Derby, the Queen Elizabeth II Cup, and the Hong Kong International Races. The 2014 winner of the Queen Elizabeth II Cup was Irish-bred Designs on Rome, ridden by Australian Tommy Berry and owned by Hong Kong native Cheng Keung Fai.

afternoon of bowling, batting, and big scores. The SAR has a national team that plays internationally and a youth team that promises a great future for cricketers.

Squash and badminton are both racket sports, and there are leagues for everyone from brand-new players to experts. The SAR holds the Hong Kong Open badminton tournament, one of the top badminton tournaments in the world. In 2008, Wang Chen, an internationally ranked female player, became the first Hong Kong player to win the gold medal at the Hong Kong Open.

Young Captain

A wicket-keeper and right-handed batter, Jamie Atkinson has represented Hong Kong's international cricket team since his teen years. Born in 1990 in Hong Kong, Atkinson became the team's youngest captain ever in 2011 at age twenty-one. Although he stepped down as captain in 2015, he remains a popular star on the cricket pitch.

Dragon Boat Races

The Tuen Ng Festival in June is a time of intense competition in the dragon boat races. The Dragon Boat Festival honors the death of Qu Yuan, a poet and hero. Protesting corrupt politicians and rulers, Qu Yuan jumped into a river and drowned. Today's dragon boat races represent efforts to rescue Qu Yuan. The races are held in many locations throughout Hong Kong during the fifth lunar month. Teams of rowers pull their paddles through the water with lightning speed. Dragon boat races are a time-honored tradition that has turned into a three-day party in Hong Kong.

Rugby is a rugged sport, similar to football, that is physical and, at times, even brutal. Hong Kongers play rugby at school and on elite teams that compete regionally and internationally. As with many other sports, both men and women have teams.

Many Hong Kongers also participate in traditional Chinese sports. At 8:00 a.m. at Tsim Sha Tsui waterfront a crowd gathers. The people bend, stretch, and glide in slow motion, much like shadowboxers. They are practicing the traditional Chinese martial art of tai chi. Hong Kongers are avid martial artists, taking part in tai chi, kung fu, and wing chun.

Arts and Crafts

The Chinese have a long history of creating fine crafts. Major craft traditions include pottery, especially working with porcelain; jade carving; silk embroidery; and calligraphy, the art of penmanship. Fine china made of porcelain includes dishes, cups, and vases. Traditionally, Chinese porcelain was white

The Hong Kong Museum
of Art has a large
collection of Chinese
calligraphy.

with hand-painted blue decoration. Now, porcelain artists use a range of colors and come from around the world to Hong Kong for the International Porcelain Painting Exhibition. They provide an outstanding display of the fine art of painting china.

At the head of Canton Road in Kowloon sits a 3-ton jade stone. It marks the entrance to Hong Kong's Jade Market, one of the biggest in the world. The Chinese character that means "jade" combines the figures for "beauty" and "purity." Jade pieces range in color from palest yellow or white to deep green.

Scissors-cut is a popular art in Hong Kong. It involves cutting a detailed design using only scissors and one piece of paper. The designs are used to decorate windows and are nicknamed *cheong fa*, or window flower. Scissors-cut artists illustrate many different subjects, from animals to mythical creatures. A scissors-cut of carp, a symbol of good luck, is placed in the doorway of a newlywed couple. Chinese characters appear in these delicate pieces, with "lucky" and "happiness" being the two most popular character designs.

Calligraphy is the art of painting Chinese characters. A fine calligraphy hand is one that can produce an entire page of writing without a single splotch or drip of ink. Chinese calligraphy is so beautiful that it is displayed in many of the world's finest museums.

The SAR is known for making fine jewelry. Some of it is mass-produced, while other pieces are handmade by gifted designers. Goldsmith Nathalie Melville produces one-of-a-kind engagement rings. Designer Marielle Byworth blends leather, stone, vinyl, and metal into bracelets and necklaces with celebrity appeal.

Living Clay

Sculptor Johnson Tsang specializes in creating works out of clay that have human qualities. A typical Tsang ceramic bowl, for example, has a human face emerging from the bottom of the bowl. Tsang, a native of Hong Kong, has won more than a dozen international awards for his work, and his art is displayed at the Hong Kong Museum of Art, the Korea Ceramic Foundation, and in private collections worldwide. Most recently, he won the Grand Prize at the 2012 Taiwan Ceramics Biennale.

The Written Word

Hong Kong is home to many novelists, poets, and journalists. Amy Siu-haan Cheung is one of Hong Kong's most popular romance writers. Hon Lai-chu has won the Biennial Award for Chinese Literature in the fiction category for his short story collection *Silent Creature*. His novels *The Kite Family* and *Gray Flower* have also gained acclaim. Despite the followings of these two major writers, they do not come close to the popularity of Hong Kong's *wuxia* writers.

Louis Cha wrote fifteen wuxia over the course of his career.

Wuxia is a genre unique to Hong Kong. It is based on martial arts stories and means literally "martial heroes." Wuxia is published as novels and short stories. It is the main genre of Hong Kong screenplays and comics. Louis Cha, better known by his pen name Jin Yong, is the best-selling Chinese author alive. His wuxia novels have sold more than 300 million copies.

Performing Arts

The curtain opens at the Hong Kong Arts Centre, and the Cantonese opera company takes the stage. The characters are classic: Man mou sang, Fa dan, Mou sang, and Chou sang. Man mou sang is the main male role, and may be young or old, and very possibly a warrior. Fa dan is the belle of the ball, a lady, an old woman, or a female warrior. Mou sang wears heavy makeup and is either a singing or an acrobatic actor, portraying a hero, a general, a villain, or a god. Chou sang is a clown and can be male or female.

Most of the people attending Cantonese opera are middle-aged or older. Younger Hong Kongers prefer to head to nightclubs

An opera performer in Hong Kong. Chinese opera began more than 1,300 years ago. At first, it was performed only for the emperor.

Joey Yung is one of the best-selling Cantopop singers.

and concert halls to hear their favorite singers and comedians perform. Cantopop, or HK-pop, is Hong Kong's version of popular music. The acts are high-tech, glitzy, and loud—just what Hong Kong teens are looking for. Screaming, enthusiastic audiences fill the Hong Kong Coliseum and other venues to see concerts by performers such as Eason Chan and Joey Yung.

Popular movies and television in Hong Kong are a mixture of original Hong Kong productions and hot picks from other parts of the world. Hong Kong movies fall into three categories: comedy, drama, and kung fu. The region's biggest star is martial arts actor Jackie Chan, but others have also made names for themselves. Recently, popular actor Donnie Yen kicked and punched his way through *Kung Fu Jungle*. Internationally known Chow Yun-fat acted in a Cantonese-language action-comedy, *From Vegas to Macau*, about a high-stakes gambler. Documentary producer Ruby Yang has won an Academy Award for her short film, *The Blood of Yingzhou District*.

Hong Kong television airs shows made locally as well as those from the United States, Australia, Korea, and other parts of China. Hong Kongers are hooked on Cantonese soap operas, sports, talk shows, and lifestyle shows. Food and travel shows are top viewing for many people, as are many of the United States' most popular TV dramas and comedies.

People in Hong Kong also keep up with the news on a daily basis. Because so many people work in the financial industry, daily news and business programs are popular. Daytime TV is filled with shows about the stock market and the financial outlook.

Martial Artist: Jackie Chan

Hong Kong native Jackie Chan is an actor, director, and producer. As a child, he studied at the Chinese Opera Research Institute, a boarding school in Hong Kong. Chan became an expert in martial arts, drama, and acrobatics. His first film, made when he was eight, was the Cantonese feature *Big and Little Wong Tin Bar* (1962). Chan worked as a stuntman and acrobat for several martial arts movies, including Bruce Lee's *Fist of Fury*. Chan has starred in dozens of films, including such Hollywood hits as *Rush Hour* and *The Karate Kid* (2010).

CHAPTER 10

Everyday Hong Kong

T IS CHINESE NEW YEAR, AND FAMILIES THROUGHOUT Hong Kong are getting ready for the celebration. This is not a one-day event, but fifteen full days packed with family events and customs tied to Chinese culture.

New Year's Eve dinner starts the celebrations. There is no school or work during the holiday, so the family has plenty of time together. Traditionally, meals begin with a fish dinner, though some families like to serve dumplings. The home is decorated with red scissors-cut decorations, and older members of the family give money in red envelopes, a color signifying good luck.

The children cannot wait for the night parade to start. Every year, brightly colored floats, marching bands, and costumed acrobats make way for the stars of the parade: the dragons. Rows of dancers carry a long dragon, making it writhe and slither down the street. The Tsim Sha Tsui parade takes about ninety minutes, and crowds cheer and jump as

Opposite: **The celebration of Chinese New Year includes parades featuring dramatic dragon dances.**

firecrackers burst on the street. Acrobats walk by on high stilts as children crane their necks to watch them. Finally, Chinese lions bring up the end of the parade, scaring away evil spirits and welcoming the New Year.

On the second day of the New Year holiday, families go as close as they can get to the waterfront. Fireworks light the night sky over the harbor. In the past, families shot off their own fireworks. In crowded Hong Kong, this is now banned for safety reasons, but the spectacular fireworks show over Victoria Harbour makes up for it.

Fireworks fill the sky over Hong Kong to celebrate Chinese New Year.

Buddha's Birthday

National Holidays

New Year's Day	January 1
Chinese Lunar New Year	January or February
Ching Ming Festival	Early April
Good Friday	March or April
Holy Saturday	March or April
Easter Monday	March or April
Buddha's Birthday	April or May
Labor Day	May 1
Dragon Boat Festival	June
Hong Kong Special Administrative Region Establishment Day	July 1
Day after Mid-Autumn Festival	September
National Day of the People's Republic of China	October 1
Chung Yeung Festival	October
Christmas Day	December 25
Boxing Day	December 26

Shoppers in Hong Kong photograph themselves with some of the decorations that cover the region during the Christmas season.

Holidays

Holidays in Hong Kong are a mix of British and Chinese traditions. On the British side, Hong Kongers celebrate New Year's Day, Easter, Christmas, and Boxing Day (the day after Christmas). Easter is a four-day event, beginning on Good Friday. Christian churches hold special services, restaurants offer Easter dinner, and bakeries and specialty shops sell hot cross buns, chocolate bunnies, and candy Easter eggs. Young children color eggs, go on Easter egg hunts, and see magic shows. All Hong Kongers, regardless of religion, enjoy having a four-day weekend and taking part in the events around the city.

Buddha's birthday became an official holiday in 1999. On this day, many people head to Lantau Island, home of the Big Buddha statue. Followers wash the statue as a sign of respect. They also eat bitter green cookies to remind them that people must pass through hardships in life.

Chung Yeung Festival

Honoring ancestors is an important part of Chinese culture and the center of the Chung Yeung Festival. On this day, many families head to local cemeteries, where they clean the graves and burn incense. Some families also go to parks where they enjoy picnics and eat *chongyang* cakes. These cakes are made from rice flour and decorated with chestnuts and almonds. They are very sweet and sticky, and children love them.

There are two annual political holidays in Hong Kong. July 1 is Hong Kong Special Administrative Region Establishment Day, which celebrates the day Hong Kong was returned to China. On October 1, people have a day off from work for National Day, which commemorates the day the People's Republic of China was founded. On both days, there are plenty of fireworks. The fireworks are presented in "acts," like a play, with different themes throughout. These themes are based on Chinese history and Chinese fictional characters.

Christmas is a two-day event, including Boxing Day on the day after Christmas. Hong Kong's Santa Claus is known as Sing Daan Lou Yan in Cantonese. Homes, businesses, and churches are decorated with paper chains, poinsettias, nativity scenes, and colored lights.

To Health

Hong Kong has long been a center for Chinese traditional medicine. For thousands of years, Chinese people have relied on the balance between yin and yang and the five basic body elements for good health. Yin and yang are the opposites in life, such as light and dark. The five body elements are fire, earth, water, metal, and wood. The interaction between yin and yang, and the interaction between the body elements determine good health. In Chinese medicine, herbs, roots, berries, animal parts, and tree bark are used to create medicines. In Sheung Wan, more than two hundred stalls and shops sell every type of medicine from dried seaweed to hornets' nests.

In addition to Chinese drugstores, many people consider *feng shui*—wind and water—an important way to keep healthy. Feng shui takes into account the way buildings and their furniture align with nearby mountains, rivers, and other buildings. Ideally, a building with good feng shui allows for a flow of good energy through its windows and doors. Good feng shui is thought to help achieve success.

The Best Time

In their everyday lives, people in Hong Kong use the same calendar that is used in the United States. But for many holidays, they use the traditional Chinese lunar calendar, which is tied to the appearance of the moon. Each Chinese year is governed by one of twelve animals: rat, ox, tiger, rabbit, dragon, snake, horse, goat, monkey, rooster, dog, or pig.

Fortune-telling and astrology are traditional Chinese customs that are popular in Hong Kong. When a couple gets engaged, it is important for the bride and groom to select a wedding date that will bring them good luck. To do this, they seek the guidance of a fortune-teller. A fortune-teller also helps people decide which job to accept, where to live, and when to travel.

Fortune-tellers use Chinese astrology and tarot cards to help them make predictions. The year a person is born is believed to affect his or her personality. Children born in the year of the monkey are expected to be fun loving. The year of the snake yields charmers, while the year of the rooster produces leaders. People born in different years have different lucky colors and numbers. For example, a child born in the year of the goat will have the lucky colors green, red, and purple. Lucky numbers for that child are two and seven, and the lucky flowers are carnations and primroses. On the other hand, the numbers three, six, and ten are unlucky, and it is best for a child born in that year to avoid important decisions during the third, sixth, and tenth months of the lunar year. People born in the year of the goat should look for love among those people born in the year of the rabbit, horse, or pig.

Each month of the lunar year is associated with a different animal.

The average woman in Hong Kong can expect to live to age eighty-seven. Men, on average, live to be eighty-one.

Good Manners

Manners are different in every country, but in Hong Kong manners tend to be traditional. Young people are expected to be polite, quiet, and respectful. Compared to Hong Kongers, people from most Western cultures might seem loud or pushy. In Hong Kong, one person greets another with a gentle handshake and the lowering of the eyes. These gestures show respect. Direct eye contact with a stranger would be too bold. In a similar way, Hong Kong Chinese do not call each other by their first names unless asked to do so.

While Hong Kongers stand fairly close to each other when speaking, they do not touch each other's bodies. A hug or a pat on the back is not acceptable. People do not start conversations with people they do not know. It is bad form to talk about politics or speak against a political viewpoint with an older person. Being loud in public and shouting or whistling is not polite behavior.

Age also plays a part in manners. Younger Hong Kongers are taught to respect their elders, and they never speak rudely to an elder or question the authority of someone older.

At Home

For Chinese people, the family is the center of life. In many cases, several generations of one family live in the same house. This is traditional, and it helps pay the bills in the increasingly expensive Hong Kong housing market. Most families live in high-rise apartment buildings. For a family of four, the apartment might have two small bedrooms. The kitchen is small, with appliances designed to fit the area. The refrigerator is smaller than a U.S. dishwasher, so the family needs to shop more often.

People often shop for food on the way home from work. Some people buy fresh fish, meat, and vegetables every couple of days. They buy staples such as rice, soy sauce, cheese, nuts, and snacks on the weekends.

Most families use public transportation, which is always crowded. By the time children are about ten years old, they take public buses or trains to school.

When children graduate from high school and begin college, the living arrangement often stays the same. Many students live at home while attending university. It is too expensive to live in a dormitory when a student can take a bus to college. Even young married couples often live with one set of parents. It costs too much to set up an apartment for only two people.

Many wealthy and middle class Hong Kongers employ Filipino or Indonesian maids. Many of these women become an important part of family life, preparing meals and taking care of children. On Sundays, their day off, the foreign workers head to Central's shopping centers and lobbies. There, they spread out blankets, have picnics, and chat with friends. Since Central Hong Kong is so densely populated, it lacks parkland, so these buildings have become public space where a festive culture has bloomed.

In the Pantry

Food in Hong Kong is quite varied. Chinese cuisine is dominant, but there are also influences from other parts of Asia, such as India and Japan, as well as from Europe. One popular food with European roots is Hong Kong egg tarts, which are

Filipino domestic workers relax in an office lobby on a Sunday. About three hundred thousand foreign domestic workers live in Hong Kong.

Hong Kong–Style Egg Tarts

Egg tarts are a delicious treat that dates back to the time when the Portuguese settled in the Hong Kong area. Have an adult help you with this recipe.

Ingredients

½ cup confectioners' sugar

1½ cups all-purpose flour

½ cup butter, softened

1 egg yolk, beaten

½ teaspoon vanilla

⅓ cup sugar

¾ cup water

5 eggs

½ cup evaporated milk

Directions

In a medium bowl, mix the confectioners' sugar and the flour. Then mix in the butter to form small crumbs. Mix in the egg yolk and ¼ teaspoon of the vanilla. Blend the mixture to form a thick dough. Break the dough into 1½-inch balls and gently press the dough into a muffin tin. The dough should line the pan like a piecrust, with the dough going slightly higher than the edge of each muffin cup. These will be the tart shells.

Next, preheat the oven to 450°F. In a medium saucepan, combine the sugar and water. Heat this mixture over medium-high heat and bring it to a boil. The sugar should be completely dissolved. Allow the mixture to cool and then whisk in the 5 eggs, one at a time, blending thoroughly. Add the evaporated milk and the other ¼ teaspoon of vanilla to the egg mixture. Fill each tart shell and bake for 15 to 20 minutes. The tarts are done when the filling looks puffy and golden brown in color. Enjoy!

By the Leaf

Chinese ties to tea go back thousands of years. According to legend, in 2737 BCE, when Emperor Shen Nung was drinking a cup of hot water in the garden, a leaf from a tea bush fell into the cup, and Shen Nung liked the flavor. The tradition of tea drinking was born. Today, Hong Kongers drink six types of tea:

- Black tea—strong flavored and reddish in color
- Compacted tea—sold in bricks or balls
- Green tea—fresh, natural, and popular
- Oolong tea—supposed to help weight loss
- Scented tea—green tea mixed with dried flower petals (rose, jasmine, orchid, or plum)
- White tea—silver color and clear in the cup

adapted from a Portuguese food. Many Hong Kongers enjoy an egg tart with tea every morning or afternoon. Tea is a regular part of life in Hong Kong. People drink it with every meal and often have tea other times of the day as well.

Rice is the basis of every Hong Kong Chinese meal, and the family's electric rice cooker is filled each evening before bedtime. For breakfast, the average Chinese Hong Konger eats rice porridge, called congee, which is rice cooked with pork, fish, vegetables, or jujubes (Chinese dates). Some people treat themselves to a Hong Kong bakery specialty—a pineapple bun, which is somewhat like a filled, sugared doughnut. A quick breakfast is a bun stuffed with pork, fish, or vegetables. When eating out, breakfast or brunch is usually dumplings, Hong Kong–style French toast (served with peanut butter or jam), or a scrambled egg sandwich.

Dim Sum

Most families eat at home during the week, but Sunday is a day for *dim sum*, a meal made of many small dishes. Families crowd into restaurants to select their favorite hot dumplings and other delicious tidbits. The meals are noisy and fun, with families greeting friends from their neighborhood at the restaurant.

Noodles are also much loved. For people who are in a hurry and need a quick meal, there is a noodle shop on nearly every street in Hong Kong. These shops have specialties, such as stuffed wontons in broth, beef tendon noodles, and noodles with prawns or shrimp. Other dishes are noodles with broiled vegetables in oyster sauce, or dry tossed prawn roe noodles. Noodles with fish balls or beef are favorites among Hong Kong natives.

Many different kinds of meat are eaten, including duck, chicken, seafood, and pork. Tofu is also common. It can be cooked, tossed in salads, or served in sweet tofu soup. It is a great source of protein and much cheaper than meat or fish.

Hot pot is a winter tradition in Hong Kong. This dish has a soup or rice base, vegetables, and meat, all cooked in one pot. Some fancy restaurants serve hot pot with rainbow colored meatballs of pork, chicken, or fish. Others make hot pot with pigs' feet.

Some of the more exotic dishes fancied by Hong Kongers are little eaten in Western countries. Chicken feet are served deep-fried and simmered in black bean sauce. Snake soup is cooked in broth with mushrooms, ginger, a butt of pork, and noodles. Lotus seed paste is sweet and nutty and is used in desserts and as the filling in white buns. In fish markets, sea cucumbers are a popular treat.

Marriage and Family

Many weddings in Hong Kong follow Chinese traditions. In a traditional marriage, the groom's family contacts the bride's family to ask about a possible marriage. At this point, the man and woman might not have even met each other. Today, that is rare, and most couples date before an engagement and a wedding. Still, a modern couple will want the approval of

Many people in Hong Kong get married wearing Western-style wedding dresses and suits.

Chinese Wedding Dress

Many Hong Kongers, even those who live very modern lives, choose to marry in a traditional Chinese wedding outfit. Brides wear a gown called a *kua-qun*. The top section is a jacket, and the bottom is a skirt. The outfit is made of nine pieces of fabric because nine in Chinese sounds the same as "long," and brides wish for long marriages. The material is red silk, the color of luck and happiness. Heavily detailed embroidery, usually in gold, covers the entire gown. The value of the dress depends on the amount of embroidery, all of which is done by hand. A kua-qun takes four months to a year to make. Because they are so expensive, many brides rent their kua-quns for a fraction of the cost of buying one.

both families before agreeing to marry. Once engaged, the Chinese zodiac is consulted for choosing a lucky day. This is true for people of all religions in Hong Kong. No one wants to start out a marriage without good luck.

On the wedding day, the groom goes to get the bride. He brings red packets with "luck money" in them, which the groom pays to the bride's family. The marriage ceremony takes place at the government registry office or in a church.

Much the same as with marriage, birth customs differ from family to family. On the whole, most Hong Kongers follow Chinese birth customs. In today's modern Hong Kong, these customs may be changed to suit the family. Having a healthy baby traditionally required that the mother be happy. Unhappy mothers made for babies that cried a lot. A mother rubbing her pregnant belly led to spoiled babies that needed

Celebrating Life

In centuries past, when a baby was born, the mother and child were expected to rest at home for a full month. New mothers ate special foods, such as pigs' feet, to regain body strength. Before modern medicine, many babies died shortly after birth, and it was believed that if a baby survived for a month, it would probably live. After a month remaining in the house, mothers and their babies went out for a full moon celebration.

Today, this custom still exists, but the party with family and friends celebrating the baby is usually held in a restaurant. The color red, for luck, is prominent at the celebration. Guests give money in red envelopes, and the feast includes plates of red hard-boiled eggs and pickled red ginger. An even number of eggs is given to guests if the baby is a girl, and an odd number of eggs is given if it's a boy.

much attention. Decorating in the home could affect a baby, so hammering, sawing, drilling, and even glue were forbidden.

A Place to Rest

In Western cultures, people mourn in black or dark clothing. In Hong Kong, the color of mourning is white. People bring flowers, fruit, or money in white envelopes to the funeral. The family eats first. Then, family members take out incense sticks and burn them to honor their loved one.

Despite their past burial traditions, Hong Kongers had to stop burying their dead in the 1980s. There simply was no room to do so. The dead are now cremated instead. Their ashes are then placed in niches in a building called a columbarium. But even these facilities are running out of room. By 2016, it is expected that there will not be enough niches for even half the people who die in Hong Kong that year.

Part of the problem has to do with feng shui. The Chinese do not believe that the living and the dead can be near each other. In tightly spaced Hong Kong, there are few other options.

For most families, scattering ashes in parks or at sea is not acceptable. The older Chinese refuse to do this. In a nation where respecting one's elders is very important, denying the ashes a final resting place goes against custom and family. The elderly wonder what will happen to the old ways as the new Hong Kong continues to grow. Hong Kongers know change must come, but giving up time-honored traditions is difficult. They know that the necessities of the living take precedence over the traditions of the dead.

A family gathers at a niche that contains the ashes of a relative.

Timeline

Stone Age settlements are established in what is now Hong Kong.	ca. 4000 BCE
During the Qin dynasty, large numbers of Chinese move to the Hong Kong area.	221–206 BCE
Many Han Chinese move to the Hong Kong region, fleeing the Mongols.	1200s
European traders arrive in Hong Kong.	Early 1500s
The East India Company begins trading in Guangzhou, north of Hong Kong.	1670s
China restricts European traders under the Canton system.	1757–1842
The British introduce opium to China.	1773
The First Opium War results in Great Britain taking over Hong Kong.	1839–1842
China fights Great Britain in the Second Opium War; the British take over Kowloon.	1856–1858

WORLD HISTORY

ca. 2500 BCE	The Egyptians build the pyramids and the Sphinx in Giza.
ca. 563 BCE	The Buddha is born in India.
313 CE	The Roman emperor Constantine legalizes Christianity.
610	The Prophet Muhammad begins preaching a new religion called Islam.
1054	The Eastern (Orthodox) and Western (Roman Catholic) Churches break apart.
1095	The Crusades begin.
1215	King John seals the Magna Carta.
1300s	The Renaissance begins in Italy.
1347	The plague sweeps through Europe.
1453	Ottoman Turks capture Constantinople, conquering the Byzantine Empire.
1492	Columbus arrives in North America.
1500s	Reformers break away from the Catholic Church, and Protestantism is born.
1776	The U.S. Declaration of Independence is signed.
1789	The French Revolution begins.

HONG KONG HISTORY

Great Britain forces China to lease it the New Territories for 99 years.	**1898**
The Chinese overthrow their Qing emperor.	**1911**
Japan invades China; refugees flee to Hong Kong.	**1937**
Japan attacks Hong Kong.	**1941**
Japan surrenders, ending World War II.	**1945**
Communist forces defeat Nationalists in China; refugees flee to Hong Kong.	**1949**
Great Britain and China sign a joint declaration concerning how Hong Kong will be governed under Chinese rule.	**1984**
Great Britain gives control of Hong Kong back to China.	**1997**
Protesters march against a law that would restrict freedom of speech.	**2003**
Protesters call for greater democratic policies in Hong Kong.	**2009**
Leung Chun-ying becomes the chief executive.	**2012**
Pro-democracy protesters occupy the central administrative district of Hong Kong.	**2014**

WORLD HISTORY

1865	The American Civil War ends.
1879	The first practical lightbulb is invented.
1914	World War I begins.
1917	The Bolshevik Revolution brings communism to Russia.
1929	A worldwide economic depression begins.
1939	World War II begins.
1945	World War II ends.
1969	Humans land on the Moon.
1975	The Vietnam War ends.
1989	The Berlin Wall is torn down as communism crumbles in Eastern Europe.
1991	The Soviet Union breaks into separate states.
2001	Terrorists attack the World Trade Center in New York City and the Pentagon near Washington, D.C.
2004	A tsunami in the Indian Ocean destroys coastlines in Africa, India, and Southeast Asia.
2008	The United States elects its first African American president.

Fast Facts

Official name: Hong Kong Special Administrative Region

Official languages: Chinese, English

Central (Victoria)

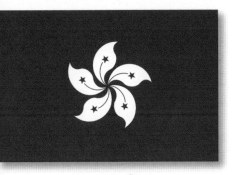
Hong Kong flag

National anthem:	"Yiyongjun Jinxingqu" ("March of the Volunteers")
Government:	Limited democracy
Head of state:	President of China
Head of government:	Chief Executive
Area of country:	427 square miles (1,105 sq km)
Highest elevation:	Mount Tai Mo, 3,140 feet (957 m)
Lowest elevation:	Sea level along the coast
Longest river:	Sham Chun, 23 miles (37 km)
Largest island:	Lantau Island, 57 square miles (148 sq km)
Tallest waterfall:	Long Falls, 115 feet (35 m)
Average daily high temperature:	64°F (18°C) in January; 90°F (32°C) in July
Average daily low temperature:	57°F (14°C) in January; 79°F (26°C) in July
Average annual precipitation:	94 inches (239 cm)
Lowest recorded temperature:	25°F (–4°C), January 18, 1893
Highest recorded temperature:	100°F (38°C), August 18, 1990

Long Falls

Hong Kong Museum of Art

National population (2014 est.): 7,112,688

Population of major urban areas (2011):

Kowloon	2,108,419
Central (Victoria)	992,221
Tsuen Wan New Town	801,800
Sha Tin New Town	630,000
Tuen Mun New Town	470,900

Landmarks:
- ▶ *Hoi Ha Wan Marine Park*, New Territories
- ▶ *Hong Kong Museum of Art*, Kowloon
- ▶ *Kadoorie Farm and Botanic Garden*, New Territories
- ▶ *Mai Po Nature Reserve*, New Territories
- ▶ *Man Mo Temple*, Sheung Wan

Economy: Services account for the vast majority of the Hong Kong economy. Hong Kong is one of the world's leading banking centers. Insurance, trade, and tourism are also important. Electronics, plastics, jewelry, and watches are all made in Hong Kong. The region also produces small amounts of fresh fruit and vegetables, poultry, pork, and fish.

Currency: The Hong Kong dollar. In 2015, $1HK equaled US$0.13, and US$1.00 equaled $7.75HK.

System of weights and measures: Chinese Qing, British imperial, and metric systems

Literacy rate (2012): 93.5%

Currency

Schoolchildren

Jackie Chan

Common Cantonese Chinese words and phrases:

neih hou	hello
funyihng	welcome
jousahn	good morning
neih hou ma	How are you?
ngoh gei hou, neih ne	I am fine, thanks.
mhgoi	thank you
joigin	good-bye

Prominent Hong Kongers:

Jamie Atkinson	(1990–)
Cricket player	
Louis Cha (Jin Yong)	(1924–)
Writer	
Jackie Chan	(1954–)
Actor and martial artist	
Li Ka-shing	(1928–)
Businessperson	
Johnson Tsang	(1960–)
Sculptor	
Tung Chee-hwa	(1937–)
First chief executive of the SAR	
Joey Yung	(1980–)
Cantopop singer	

To Find Out More

Books

▶ Debnam, Mio. *Hong Kong: Tell Your Parents Where to Go*. Port St. Lucie, FL: Haven Books, 2011.

▶ Nunes, Shiho. *Chinese Fables: "The Dragon Slayer" and Other Timeless Tales of Wisdom*. North Clarendon, VT: Tuttle Publishing, 2013.

▶ Wangu, Madhu Bazaz. *Buddhism*. New York: Facts on File, 2009.

Music

▶ Chan, Eason. *Don't Want to Let Go*. Phantom Sound & Vision, 2008.

▶ *Hong Kong: Instrumental Music*. Paris, France: UNESCO, 2015.

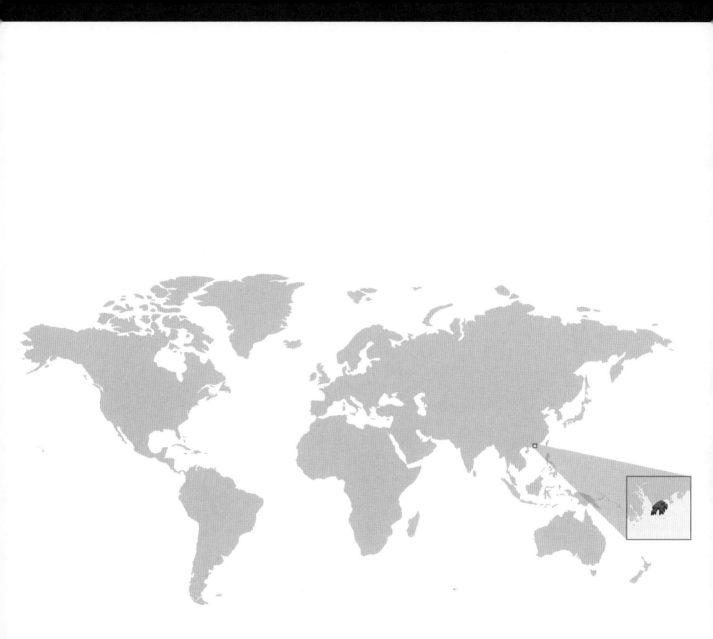

▶ Visit this Scholastic Web site for more information on Hong Kong:
www.factsfornow.scholastic.com
Enter the keywords **Hong Kong**

Index

Page numbers in *italics* indicate illustrations.

service industries, 72, 73–74
Standard Chartered Bank, 77
taxes, 86
tourism, 37, 39, 41, *41*, 55, 74, 90
trade, 43–44, 46–47, *47*, 48, 49,
   50, 52, 74, 76
trade unions, 61
Tung Chee-hwa and, 58
wealth gap, 78
ecotourism, 41
education, 71, 84–85, *85*, 86, 87–89,
   88, 96, 109, 119
egg tarts, 120, *121*, *121*, 122
elderly people, 80, 118, *118*, 127
elections, 58, 60, 62, 64, 66
employment, 61, *70*, *75*, 77–78, 84, 89
endangered species, 29
English language, 79, 84, 89, 90–91,
   91
English Schools Foundation, 84
Environmental Protection
   Department (EPD), 24
executive branch of government, 58,
   58, 61, 62–63, *62*
Executive Council, 62–63

F

families, 10, 45, *45*, 78, 86, 89, 111,
   112, 115, *115*, 119, 123, 124, 125,
   126, 127, *127*
feng shui (wind and water), 116,
   126–127
ferret badgers, 34
ferries, *81*
Filipino people, 83, 97, 119, *120*
financial services industry, 69, *70*, 71,
   73
fireworks, 112, *112*, 115
First Opium War, 49–50
fishing industry, 76–77
Fist of Fury (movie), 109
flooding, 24

foods, 12, *12*, 35, *35*, 43, 83, 84, 87,
   87, 88, 91, 111, 114, 115, 119,
   120, 121, *121*, 122–124, *123*, 126
forests, 20, 22, *26*, 30, 35, 36, 38, 40,
   40, 43, *74*
fortune-telling, 10, *10*, 116–117
France, 52
From Vegas to Macau (movie), 109
full moon celebrations, 126
functional constituencies, 66
funeral customs, 126–127, *127*

G

geography
   borders, 20, 21, 24, *24*
   Bride's Pool, 23
   Cape D'Aguilar, 18, *18*
   coastline, *16*, 19, *41*
   Dragon's Back ridge, 18
   elevation, 18, 19, 22
   Hong Kong Island, 18
   Inspiration Lake, 19, 23
   islands, 17, 18, 19, 21, *21*
   Kowloon, 17, 20, 44
   land area, 17, 19
   land reclamation, 20, 27
   Lantau Island, 19, 21, *21*
   Lion Rock, 20–21, *20*
   Long Falls, 19
   Mirror Pool, 23
   Mount Tai Mo, 19, 22, *22*, 25, 26
   New Territories, 21, 44
   Sham Chun River, 19, 24, *24*
   Victoria Peak, 18, 50, 69
   volcanoes, 22, *23*
   waterfalls, 19, *19*, 23
   Wong Leng peak, 22
Goldfish Market, 14
government
   Basic Law, 61–62, 67
   births and, 86
   chief executives, 58, *58*, 62, *62*, 133

China and, 17, 59, 61, 62, *62*
conservation, 38, 40–41
Court of Appeal of the High
   Court, 66, 67
Court of Final Appeal, 66, 67
Court of First Instance, 67
Court of First Instance of the High
   Court, 66
Daoguang (emperor), 49, *49*
district councils, 68
District Court, 67
economy and, 58, 62
ecotourism and, 41
education and, 86
elections, 58, 60, 62, 64, 66
emperors, 48, 49, *49*
Environmental Protection
   Department (EPD), 24
executive branch, 58, *58*, 61,
   62–63, *62*
Executive Council, 62–63
flooding and, 24
functional constituencies, 66
Government House, 51
Great Britain and, 67
housing and, 84
judicial branch, 61, 63, 66–67,
   66, 91
juvenile courts, 67
language and, 90
laws, 62
legislative branch, 58, 61, 63, 64,
   64, 66
Legislative Council, 58, 63, 64,
   64, 66
Magistrates' Courts, 67
manners and, 118
marriage and, 125
Mega Events Fund, 74
pollution and, 24, 37
protests, 58–59, *59*
religion and, 61

Meet the Author

ARBARA SOMERVILL HAS
been writing children's nonfiction
books for more than twenty years.
She writes about countries, earth
science, biographies, and social
studies. Somervill also teaches
college writing and critical read-
ing classes. When not teaching or
writing, she loves movies, theater,
baking, and women's softball.

Photo Credits

Photographs ©:

cover: Igor Demchenkov/Shutterstock, Inc.; back cover: Merten Snijders/Getty Images; 2: Vichaya Kiatying-Angsulee/Alamy Images; 5: Felix Lipov/Alamy Images; 6 left: Mark Hannaford/Getty Images; 6 center: Ian Trower/Robert Harding Picture Library/Superstock, Inc.; 6 right: winhorse/iStockphoto; 7 left: themorningglory/Shutterstock, Inc.; 7 right: leungchopan/Shutterstock, Inc.; 8: Sean Gallagher/National Geographic Creative; 10: LOOK Die Bildagentur der Fotografen GmbH/Alamy Images; 12: Wiskerke/Alamy Images; 13: Vidler Steve/Prisma/Superstock, Inc.; 15: BonkersAboutTravel/Alamy Images; 16: Leung Cho Pan/Dreamstime; 18: David Wong/Getty Images; 19: Ron Yue/Alamy Images; 20: themorningglory/Shutterstock, Inc.; 21: bunlee/Shutterstock, Inc.; 22: Matthew Wellings/Alamy Images; 23: Leung Cho Pan/Dreamstime; 24: chrisstockphotography/Alamy Images; 25: Alex Hofford/EPA/Landov; 26: keng po leung/Alamy Images; 27 top: itpow/Thinkstock; 27 bottom: cozyta/Shutterstock, Inc.; 28: FLPA/Alamy Images; 30: Michael Pitts/Minden Pictures; 31: FLPA/Superstock, Inc.; 32 top: Wong Hock weng/Alamy Images; 32 bottom: Yurikr/Dreamstime; 33: Paul Rushton/Alamy Images; 34: MikeLane45/iStockphoto; 35: Pixel 8/Alamy Images; 36 top: Sam Yue/Alamy Images; 36 bottom: jorender/iStockphoto; 37: Michael Pitts/Minden Pictures; 38: Juniors Bildarchiv GmbH/Alamy Images; 39 top: leungchopan/Shutterstock, Inc.; 39 bottom: Chi Wai Li/Dreamstime; 40 top: nitinut380/Shutterstock, Inc.; 40 bottom: Anny Chan/Shutterstock, Inc.; 41: Mark Hannaford/Getty Images; 42, 44: VH/age fotostock; 45: Foto 28/Alamy Images; 46: Musee du Berry, Bourges, France/Bridgeman Images; 47: Pictures From History/The Image Works; 48: North Wind Picture Archives; 49: Pictures From History/The Image Works; 51: Alinari Archives/The Image Works; 53: North Wind Picture Archives/The Image Works; 54: Robert Hunt Library/Mary Evans/The Image Works; 55: akg-images/Paul Almasy/Newscom; 56: Pictures From History/The Image Works; 57: STR/Getty Images; 58: M.N.Chan/Getty Images; 59: Lewis Tse Pui Lung/Shutterstock, Inc.; 60: Lui Siu Wai/Xinhua Press/Corbis Images; 62: Xinhua/Alamy Images; 64: Lui Siu Wai/Xinhua/Landov; 65: Joe Fox/age fotostock/Superstock, Inc.; 66: Bobby Yip/Reuters/Landov; 67: Atlaspix/Shutterstock, Inc.; 68: Monkey Business Images/Shutterstock, Inc.; 69: leungchopan/Shutterstock, Inc.; 70: Colin Galloway/Alamy Images; 72: Alex Hofford/EPA/Landov; 73: LatitudeStock/Capture Ltd/Superstock, Inc.; 75: Rick Friedman/Corbis Images; 76: Mosessin/Dreamstime; 77: Casper1774 Studio/Shutterstock, Inc.; 79: Ton Koene/age fotostock/Superstock, Inc.; 80 top: KreangchaiRungfamai/iStockphoto; 80 bottom: Bloomberg/Getty Images; 81: cozyta/Shutterstock, Inc.; 82: Jerome Favre/EPA/Landov; 85: Sean Sprague/The Image Works; 86: YM Yik/EPA/Newscom; 87 top: XiXinXing/Alamy Images; 87 bottom: Casarsa/Getty Images; 88: Jeffrey Greenberg/The Image Works; 89: Lee Snider/The Image Works; 90: J.D. Dallet/Getty Images; 91: age fotostock/Superstock, Inc.; 92: leungchopan/Shutterstock, Inc.; 94: Lee Snider/The Image Works; 95: gong hangxu/iStockphoto; 96: typhoonski/iStockphoto; 97: e X p o s e/Shutterstock, Inc.; 99: Jeffrey Greenberg/The Image Works; 100: Victor Fraile/Corbis Images; 102 top: Vince Caligiuri/Getty Images; 102 bottom: Munir Uz Zaman/Getty Images; 103: Ian Trower/Robert Harding Picture Library/Superstock, Inc.; 104: Lyndon Giffard Images/Alamy Images; 106: Imaginechina/Corbis Images; 107: Runstudio/Getty Images; 108: Top Photo Corporation/Alamy Images; 109: Moviestore collection Ltd/Alamy Images; 110: Robert Harding Picture Library/Superstock, Inc.; 112: winhorse/iStockphoto; 113: Moon Yin Lam/Alamy Images; 114: Bloomberg/Getty Images; 115: Alain Evrard/Impact/HIP/The Image Works; 117: Charles Walker/TopFoto/The Image Works; 118: Jess Yu/Dreamstime; 120: Rob Crandall/The Image Works; 121: Shutter_M/Shutterstock, Inc.; 122: Media Bakery; 123: Lucas Vallecillos/Iberfoto/The Image Works; 124: Lee Snider/The Image Works; 125: Lau Chun Kit/Shutterstock, Inc.; 127: AFP/Getty Images; 130: leungchopan/Shutterstock, Inc.; 131 top: Atlaspix/Shutterstock, Inc.; 131 bottom: Ron Yue/Alamy Images; 132 top: Lyndon Giffard Images/Alamy Images; 132 bottom: Casper1774 Studio/Shutterstock, Inc.; 133 bottom: Moviestore collection Ltd/Alamy Images; 133 top: Sean Sprague/The Image Works.

Maps by XNR Productions, Inc.